THE *ALTERNATIVE*

Most of what you believe about poverty is wrong

Mauricio L. Miller

ISBN: 978-1-4834-7225-6 (sc)
ISBN: 978-1-4834-7226-3 (hc)
ISBN: 978-1-4834-7224-9 (e)

Library of Congress Control Number: 2017910152

Artist Credit: Nicholas Lim

Lulu Publishing Services rev. date: 7/14/2017

To my mother, Berta

How Most People Saw Her	How She Should Have Been Seen
Mexican immigrant	Learned math & bookkeeping on her own
Underemployed	Worked two jobs and did side work
Single mom	Talented dress designer and seamstress
Twice divorced	Became a U.S. citizen
3rd Grade Education	Put her son thru UC Berkeley, engineering
Daughter in trouble	Assured daughter was cared for by her son

CONTENTS

SECTION II

The Alternative
Put families in the driver's seat

INTRODUCTION
Disrupting the deficit view

Berta only attended school through the third grade. In the Mexico of her era that was not rare. When two divorces left her ostracized by many in her small Catholic town of Nogales, Mexico, she was left with two young children, no money, and no marketable skills. Seeking a fresh start, she immigrated to the U.S. where her daughter became a teen mother at the age of sixteen. The mounting stress of this life taxed her health, leaving her with bleeding ulcers among other maladies.

Hearing this story of Berta's life you may feel sorry for her but conclude, nonetheless, that her troubles were ultimately the result of poor decisions. In national conversations those at one end of the political spectrum would argue that her story is another example of why we need to stop Mexican immigrants from coming to the U.S.; the other side might view her as a victim in need of help from the professional social service sector. Both of these viewpoints exemplify the prevailing deficit view[1] of most

---

1 Refer to the Notes at the end of the book for citations and links to many of the terms and research cited throughout the book.

1

families that cycle in and out of poverty.

So what is the reality of Berta's story? Like the vast majority of the working poor she was smart, creative, and amazingly determined. She was self-taught in math and English and enlisted a friend to teach her bookkeeping so she could get a job. A great seamstress with a natural talent for design she envisioned and made dresses to make money on the side. Determined to make a better life for her children she saved enough to find the fastest growing city in California, and moved there. She put her kids into good schools, worked two jobs, and saved to get her son into and through U.C. Berkeley as an engineer. Yes, there was drama and trauma but, my God, this woman, my mother, was to be admired and trusted, not pitied.

She wanted to be recognized for her talents and hard work. Don't we all? My mother left Mexico because she believed that hard work and talent was rewarded in the United States. She wasn't looking for charity. Yet once here she discovered she was viewed in a stereotypical way that limited her potential. She had expected to encounter those who were racist and sexist, those who would try to put her down. What surprised her is that even those who wanted to be helpful classified her as a charity case, distrusting her decisions, even those as a parent. As was also true for her friends, my mother's pride would not accept being labeled a charity case.

This book provides a glimpse of how those who wash our dishes, pick our food, and guard our buildings, see themselves. And it proposes how recognizing people's resourcefulness, rather than their deficits, can lead to an *alternative* system of investment in their lives that expands our economy and builds a stronger tomorrow for everyone.

The *alternative* is not a program so it is important to understand that the program described here, the Family Independence Initiative, FII, was set up primarily to demonstrate that *disempowering* programs, so that families can lead their own change, will actually lead to better outcomes. FII has been called the "un-program" since it provides no services. I also have to acknowledge that while most of the critiques here are aimed at the social service sector, they are not meant to bolster the right wingers or racists. Instead this is a challenge to those that want to bring about a fundamental change to current social service approaches. Those who want to take on the mantle of closing the income and wealth gap must disrupt current practices that are based on looking for people's weaknesses and instead invest directly in low-income families, based on their initiative.

In letter to other pastors, while in the Birmingham jail, Martin Luther King, Jr. wrote:

"I have almost reached the regrettable conclusion that the Negro's great stumbling block in his stride toward freedom is not the White Citizen's Counciler or the Ku Klux Klanner, but the white moderate." Noting their paternalism, he continued, "Shallow understanding from people of good will is more frustrating than absolute misunderstanding from people of ill."

Today most *poverty experts,* of any color, have a very shallow understanding of life in poverty and they promote a view of families like mine as somehow deficient. These experts highlight only the data or stories that backs a deficit view of low-income families.

Our helping system for the poor is based on charity, on well-meaning outsiders saving the poor. But the stories, data, and research presented here shows that charity slows progress. It is actually a barrier to its own mission. A focus on weaknesses hides talent and potential. There are embedded solutions and leaders in the very communities these experts seek to help. If, instead, they focused on the strengths of low-income families we would all see they are important contributors to society and as such we should invest in their talents, much as our society invests in the rich.

My story, like that of the other families I will present here, illustrates the complexity faced by those living at the bottom of our economy, as well as the resourcefulness these families display. These are stories not of exceptional families, but altogether typical ones. Census studies, that will be cited in chapter two, have continually showed that only around 3 percent, not 15 percent, of our population stays in poverty for more than a few years, with an average stay of only six months as people find work again after each layoff or cut in hours. We simply don't have a large, stagnant, underclass that needs to be saved or deserves to be called lazy. *Most of what our society believes about poverty is wrong.*

The alternative being proposed is simply that if we recognize and invest in the talents and initiatives low-income families demonstrate every day — if we look for those traits rather than their deficits — we can create an investment system that helps those efforts grow, which benefits all of us. We can break the cycle of poverty. By highlighting the contributions of low-income families we also begin to challenge some of the racist, classist, and gender-based prejudice that continues to divide our country.

My journey to understanding the depth of the *deficit view,* as well as the *alternative* view, began with the challenge that my mother issued to me when I was ten years old. A challenge to not let what was happening to our family happen to others. It's a journey that would take me through U.C.

Berkeley, the Vietnam War, a long career in the nonprofit sector, honors from two U.S. Presidents, and hundreds of mothers like my own.

*

A chance to start over

"The White House is calling", my receptionist yelled down the hall. It had to be a joke but she did sound excited. I picked up the phone and a woman from the office of the President's chief of staff said, "President Clinton would like to invite you to his upcoming State of the Union Address to honor the community work you do."

It was December 1998, and I was at a personal low point. For twenty years the nonprofit social service agency I ran had provided job training and support to hundreds of young men and women, yet I was now seeing the children of my first trainees showing up and still needing the same services. It was increasingly clear to me that my work wasn't fundamentally changing things for the families I had been trying to help.

Just as I knew that my work wasn't really working, I also knew that my mother would never have utilized the services I offered. She would have considered them patronizing. To qualify for my programs people had to highlight their weaknesses, their deficiencies. The more helpless you presented yourself to be, the more eligible you were for services. My mother had hated that. She, like most of the families I grew up with, wanted to be recognized for their strengths, good deeds, and hard work. She refused to compete to look more needy than her neighbor. A system to help that was primarily built to look for deficits was a fundamentally flawed approach and I knew it, so why would the President want to invite me to anything important? I had never watched a State of the Union address[2] so I had no idea what I was being invited to. I was supposed to be in the Philippines on the date of the President's speech, meeting the father I'd never known. My parents divorced when I was two and I had never heard from him. Through a set of fortunate accidents, however, I had discovered that he was living in Manila[3] and I had planned on bringing my kids to meet him. Not understanding the significance of the invitation, I told the White House staffer that unfortunately I was busy. She seemed surprised and kept pressing me.

"Are you *sure* you can't come?" she asked several times before giving up.

Her persistence made me wonder. After I hung up the phone, I stared at it and then called my wife. "Did I do something stupid?" I asked. My wife was not one for emotional responses, but her long pause told me everything I needed to know. Then she asked in a measured tone, "Did the White House really invite you to the State of the Union Address, and did you *really* turn them down?"

"Well, uh, yes," I answered, beginning to feel a little sheepish.

"You know I can change our flight to Manila. I don't think your father would mind our changing plans so you can meet the President." It hadn't crossed my mind that I would meet the President. "Call them back and tell them we want to go!" she insisted.

"So, is this a big deal or something?" I asked, still confused.

---

2   The State of the Union address is a speech presented by the President of the United States to a joint session of the United States Congress. Since 1982 when President Ronald Reagan invited Lenny Skutnik to recognize his act of heroism, more everyday Americans have been invited.

3   Just as the call from the White House was a bit of serendipity, finding my father was also. One of the few things I knew about my father's family was my grandfather's name. It turned out that my wife's father in Cleveland had a friend from China, now living in Manila, that he asked to help me. Strangely out of the 13 million people in Metro Manila he happened to have gone to the same church as my grandfather, recognized his name, and was able to connect us in about 20 minutes.

"Big deal? The President invites only ten or twelve people a year to the speech — from the whole country! Yes, it's a big deal."

When I finally got Clara Shin from the White House back on the phone I told her that I would like to go, that is, if she hadn't already gone to the next person on the list. She laughed. "There is no next person. No one has ever turned us down. Rosa Parks and Sammy Sosa are two of the other guests."

So I went. I postponed my trip to Manila to see my father, and some weeks later I sat in the gallery of the House of Representatives, a couple rows behind Hillary Clinton and Rosa Parks. President Clinton was dealing with the Monica Lewinsky incident but he walked into the hall that night as if he owned the place. It was impressive. We were told that the President might mention some of the invitees since each of us represented a part of his speech, but he didn't call me out.

My invitation reflected the President's interest in economic development and some of our results were considered impressive. On average, graduates of our program experienced an income increase of 8 percent and they typically held their jobs for over a year. What few people knew, however, was that it cost almost $15,000 per person to get those results[4]. I had already done the math. If, instead, I took that $15,000 and divided it over ten years I could have guaranteed my trainee a 10 percent income increase for ten years. I worried my program was doing more to employ professional trainers than secure the future of our clients. The President didn't mention me, which was just as well, given how secretly disappoint-

---

4   In the 1990's it cost our agency $8,000 per student to teach construction over a 16-week period. Graduates from most training programs failed to keep the jobs they were placed in for a variety of reasons and so we spent another $7,000 to provide support services (driving them to work at times, etc.) for a year so that they would keep the job.

ed I was in my work.

The evening ended with a reception in the East Room of the White House where I met Whoopi Goldberg and had a nice chat with actress Mary Steenburgen. The President was busy talking with Jesse Jackson a few feet away. Then the twelve speech invitees met privately with the President and First Lady. Bill Clinton congratulated me for all my good work, while giving me his signature you-are-the-most-important-person-in-the-world handshake and smile. I didn't have the courage to tell him that if he considered my anti-poverty work as among the best in the country, our national standards were too low.

My life floats between two worlds, one of privilege, and one of poverty. Growing up in a poor household, my family was viewed as less than capable; now, here in the White House, I was seen as smart — except of course for my dumb move of almost turning down the invitation. Yet I was the exact same person all along. That's why character judgments based on socio-economic status really bother me. Going back and forth between these two worlds made me aware of how people's perceptions, the stereotypes they hold, affect the opportunities that are offered.

Our society assumes that people with money should have a range of choices to shape their lives and the freedom to explore them. *Choice is so American.* Now as part of the middle class I expect others to respect my decisions about my life, and even accept that I make mistakes. In the world of poverty, my clients, like my own family members, are granted few choices and certainly no respect. As a university graduate people want to see my talents and ideas and sometimes are willing to invest in them. I have won fellowships and awards. But no one wanted to see what a talented designer and seamstress my mother was. The social service sector's helping system seeks to address the deficits in people's lives. I was feeling trapped in my service agency and wished I could start all over again.

To my surprise the opportunity to try something entirely new arrived about nine months after my visit to Washington. I was eating dinner when my home phone rang. Jerry Brown, then mayor of Oakland and future Governor of California, was on the line. He wasn't happy. I didn't know him well but I could tell that he was pissed off. He wanted to talk about an agency on whose board I sat, the Oakland Private Industry Council. It was applying for grants to bring $10.2 million dollars in youth programs to Oakland.

"Do you know about this?" he demanded sternly.

I was aware of the proposal, but as a board member I hadn't seen the actual document. Still, it would mean a lot of money for Oakland. Most mayors would have been thrilled. Not Jerry Brown. Although it was seven in the evening he had an aide drive the proposal to my house and waited for me to read it and call him back. I turned to the budget section to see how the money would be spent. The plan was to use the $10.2 million grant from the U.S. Department of Labor to hire 120 social workers, employment specialists, and administrators as well as open three new youth centers. I swallowed hard and called him back.

"Are you looking at it? Doesn't this look like poverty pimping to you?" he blasted. The term stung.

The phrase echoed back to a Black Panther rally I attended in 1966 on the U.C. Berkeley campus when the Panthers claimed that President Lyndon Johnson's War on poverty would create jobs for professional helpers, not for them. They called it poverty pimping[5].

Mayor Brown had a point about the proposal. I shuffled through a few more pages to see what spending all this money would accomplish. Although 120 professionals would be assured jobs, the outcomes for the youth were only "hopes." We "hope" some youth get jobs, we "hope" more stay in school, we "hope" that fewer end up in jail and so on. I wasn't about to argue the poverty pimp label with Jerry. Like other nonprofit leaders I blamed the lack of fundamental change on having too little money and too many restrictions. He countered that after thirty years of a war on poverty the social service sector's primary accomplishment was to made living in poverty more tolerable for some. I quietly agreed. My mother didn't come to America to live in tolerable poverty.

To this day I don't know why Jerry Brown called me. I have no idea how he found my home number. I don't know why he singled me out from the other seventeen board members. But the next thing he said changed my life.

"Look," he said sternly. "If you could do anything you wanted to do, if money or restrictions were not a problem, what would you do to actually make a difference? My aide will set up an appointment for you to come next month and show me!" And with that he hung up.

His challenge was a flash of freedom, like being let out of jail. Growing up poor I had gotten accustomed to being boxed in, but here was the mayor urging me to think and dream big. Was there an alternative path? For two weeks, I wracked my brain for ideas from my past and from my experiences running social service programs. But all this freedom of

---

5   The term poverty pimping suggests that those labeled as such unduly profit from the misfortune of others. There's an implication that they are less willing to eliminate the problem as it threatens their careers.

thought forced me to admit that I didn't know what to do. All I had was my mother's story.

The following month I stood opposite Mayor Brown, tall, lean, and balding, as he shouted orders to his team. Meeting with Jerry was always stimulating and somewhat surreal. He stood, apparently distracted, behind a huge cluttered desk, but I knew the moment was coming when his eyes and attention would focus on me. It was like President Clinton's laser stare in the Blue Room of the White House. Where do politicians learn to do this?

He turned to me and with no greeting he asked, "So, what would you do?"

"Well, I don't know what *I* would do," I told him hesitantly. "But my mother figured out what to do to get *me* out of poverty, and I think every mother, father or guardian will know the best way to get their own families' lives together. Just as you challenged me, I would challenge those families to show us what they would do to build their own lives. I would flip the whole thing. Instead of paying staff, let's pay the families to show us what they would do. I'm sure we will learn something new."

I half expected to be thrown out but instead you could see the Mayor's mind playing with that image. I took that opportunity to add. "I have been studying our history, how Harlem and the Chinatowns were built, and how the Irish and others came to dominate certain occupations. It took friends coming together and helping one another, referring one another into jobs. Instead of employing social workers as helpers, I will enroll groups of families who are friends so they can help each other. I think it takes a group to get out of poverty, not a program," I declared feeling a bit more confident as he listened.

"I already have a data collection and journaling system," I continued. "If we put it online we can get the families to report what they do for themselves and others. Instead of collecting data about what families *don't* do, I want to collect stories and data on their initiative. We will learn from their perspective what works and doesn't work." He seemed interested.

"There will be no counselors, trainers, or programs. We will go directly to the families to see what they do. From the funds we save by not hiring social workers, we will provide resources directly to families based on what they do for themselves and others. I will audit the data they give us. I promise to pick the same families I normally see coming through our programs. I won't primarily enroll those that are likely to succeed."

Even though I had been running social welfare programs in Oakland and San Francisco for twenty years, now I was proposing no program involving professional social workers and trainers. The mayor only asked a few questions but had his longtime aide, Jacques Berzaghi, finish questioning me. Finally the Mayor threw his weight behind this unique experiment; letting families lead their own strategies for change.

The project I proposed, which I called the Family Independence Initiative, FII, was set up to look at families through a lens focused on their strengths rather than their deficiencies and weaknesses. It would mimic the opportunity that Jerry Brown was providing to me. Jerry asked me how I would solve the problem so I would in turn ask the families how they would go about changing their lives. Just as he didn't attempt to lead my effort but instead trusted me to shape and lead it, I would depend on the families to lead their change. He backed my efforts — which is the only way I got funding to do the work — and so I would back the efforts of families and try to get them direct access to the resources they needed to change their lives. Social service professionals would *not* play a role.

The alternative that FII was set to demonstrate skips government and nonprofit programs and instead gets dollars directly to the families as they take initiative. This new approach encourages families to turn to friends — social capital[6] — not professional staff for help and advice. FII was set up to gather the proof points to show that if we trust the families to lead their own change, that their solutions are more effective and sustainable. FII is not the only approach that can be set up which can allow families to lead their own change, but over the last fifteen years of testing, the Family Independence Initiative is proving the following:

1. That families like mine are not in this country for charity — or to be criminals. People are not happy on welfare and don't want to live in tolerable poverty. As my mother and sister would often say "If they just gave me a fraction of what they spend trying to help me, we would be so much better off".

2. FII is also proving that when friends work together to improve their lives, their example becomes contagious and leads to faster and more effective social change than starting more programs or passing policies and legislation.

3. Lastly, that this new approach rewards hard work, resourcefulness, and thus expands everyone's contributions to society. This *alternative* incorporates aspects that will be attractive to people across the political spectrum, bringing all of us together.

---

6   Social capital refers to relationships or social networks that are marked by reciprocity, trust and cooperation. There are a number of terms used in the book that are considered "jargon" within the field of social services.

*

The first section of this book will chronicle the lessons I have gained through my experiences about the flaws in our current helping system. In the second section I will share what I have learned from other families about how this country can establish and restore socio-economic mobility.

SECTION I

A Fundamentally Flawed Social Service System

CHAPTER ONE

The Challenge
No pity parties here

Born in northern Mexico with the last name Miller (German immigrants also helped colonize Mexico), my mother Berta was proud of her
Mexican heritage. She often said that pride comes from respecting yourself, your family, and your culture.   When I was a child, friends and even
strangers would comment on how beautiful my mother was. Behind a quiet exterior, she was strong willed, independent, and street smart. She was
only 5' 1", but she carried herself as if she were a foot taller, with that
sense of entitlement that you mostly see in rich people. "I should have
been born rich," she often commented. *If only.*

Growing up under her wing, I experienced two different views of her.
To me she was the smartest, most determined person in the world. However, since we were poor, others would default to a negative stereotype
of her. If you are a parent with very little income and struggling, the pre-

vailing belief is that it must be your fault. Those who are better off infer that you are lazy, dumb, or dependent on government. More charitable outsiders might see you as a victim that society must lead out of the abyss of poverty. My mother and most everyone we knew were far from dumb or helpless.

My father was Chinese from the Philippines. He had a dominating and controlling personality and clashed with my mother, often. He expected her, as a woman, to be subservient, but it wasn't in her nature. When I turned two, she asked my father for a divorce and sole custody of me. My father agreed to the divorce but he insisted that he was going to take me away from her. My half-sister, from my mother's first marriage, remembers my mother's cries and desperation.

My mother was determined not to give me up, so she devised a risky plan. She complained to people that my father was abusive and that she was afraid of him. Since he was a foreigner, many in our small town of Nogales, Mexico, were already suspicious of him. Then one afternoon she called her brother Mario to come up the hill to our house. As he got out of his car and approached the house, she took the gun my father kept for protection and shot herself in the lower abdomen. I saw the scar growing up. Mario ran into the house to find my mother crumpled on the floor, bleeding. He put her in the car and drove her to the hospital. The laws in Mexico at that time were somewhat fluid, so when she recovered, she charged my father with attempted murder!

Many years later, I found my father's trial written up in the front pages of *Accion*, the Nogales newspaper. The articles describe how she convinced a judge that my father psychologically abused her, threatened to never let her see me, pushed her into shooting herself, and gave her the

18

gun. When she did shoot herself, he heard the shot and didn't try to save her. My father's side of the story is that since his family had money the judge wanted to shake him down, but on principle he wouldn't pay the judge off. My father was convicted and sent to jail and my mother now had custody of me.

From jail, my father sold the tungsten mine his family owned and used his money to get a new trial with a higher court. After a year in jail, he was exonerated. Wisely, however, he decided he didn't want to fight my mother anymore, left me with her, and returned to the Philippines, where I found him just before my invitation to the State of the Union address. From this point on, my half-sister Raquel and I were hers, and she took control of our lives as best she could. She was not about to let anyone tell her how to raise her children.

I feel my mother's story is extraordinary, but I have learned it is also somewhat typical. My family's story illustrates the extent to which parents are willing to go for their children. We see this initiative in immigrants and refugees as well as those who continue to fight the legacy of slavery and racism. But these stories are hidden and instead those in poverty or crisis are viewed as incapable, a drain on society, or even uncaring of their children. As a presidential candidate, Donald Trump revealed the prejudice held by so many in society against women and various ethnic and religious groups, people who view these groups monolithically and believe they don't contribute to society. What they don't see is that it takes a lot more smarts and resourcefulness to survive with no money than it does when you are rich or privileged. Rather than lazy or victims waiting for saviors, low-income parents are creative, innovative, determined, and resourceful. The *alternative* I present here focuses on people's strengths and contributions.

*

The journey begins

I had just turned nine years old when my mother announced to my half-sister Raquel and me that we were moving to the United States, to San Jose, California. She had saved three hundred dollars by doing bookkeeping and sewing. Then, with no job, no friends in San Jose, and no place to stay, she bought the three of us seats on a Greyhound bus — one way — and we headed north.

I was both excited and scared to go on this adventure. I have almost no memory of our years in Nogales, but the chain of memories starts like gang-busters on that bus. Raquel made friends with everyone, and as the bus rolled, she had everyone singing the greatest hits from the 1950s. I was too shy to join her so I just watched and looked out the window as a new world swished by.

We arrived in San Jose at dusk the following day. As we stepped off the bus, I anxiously asked Mom where we were going to sleep. She waved off my question with a flick of her wrist, and then, instructing Raquel and me to stay with the luggage, she strode off to the yellow cabs that were lined up outside the bus station. I watched as she carefully bent down and looked at each of the drivers, finally stopping at one. She turned quickly toward us and motioned for us to bring the luggage. As I got near the cab I heard her tell the driver, "I've looked at every driver here, and you are the one I feel I can trust. I have two young children and I need you to take us to a motel that is safe but not expensive."

Without waiting for an answer, she ushered us into the cab as the startled driver realized our fate was in his hands. To his credit and my mother's instincts, he took us to a nice motel just on the outskirts of San Jose. And that is where life started for us again. *America held so much promise in that moment.*

The next day Mom collected the newspapers and went out to find work. We all thought — and might still think today — that a woman this smart and determined could accomplish anything. But the reality of being poor in America hit quickly. By the third day, she was pacing in our room. I could feel her frustration. Though she spoke perfectly good English, she was realizing that it was not enough.

"They hear my accent and then ask me where I'm from," she said of the people interviewing her. "Then they stop asking important questions. They think Mexicans are lazy and dirty, so from now on we don't speak Spanish any more. I have to get rid of my accent."

Hiding her cultural background ate at her, but she needed work. This was the reality in the 1950s that too often continues today. I don't know if hiding that she was Mexican helped — at times she told people she was from India — but Mom finally did get a job as a bookkeeping clerk at the local Nash automobile dealership. She also took a second job in the evening at a grocery store.

We were finally able to move into our first apartment at 708 North First Street in San Jose. It was an immense achievement. We celebrated by jumping up and down on the bed and dancing hand in hand.[7] But the bouncing had to stop when the neighbor below us knocked on our door and told us that we were shaking her chandelier! Afraid to be evicted from

---

7   In the movie Seven Pounds there is a scene exactly like this; a Latina mom celebrating their new home with her two children. The feelings emoted in that scene are exactly how we felt.

our first home in America, we tiptoed around the apartment from then on.

Life in a new country required a balance of conflicting needs and aspirations. The location of our apartment meant that my sister and I would go to good schools, but the rent was higher than in other parts of town, so we were told we would have to give up other things like extra clothes, presents, and desserts. Mom would take the bus to work as she saved for a car, and my sister had to watch over me.

Raquel, who was six years older than me, was enrolled in a good high school and I was enrolled in Belden Elementary School. Raquel got a job working after school, but as the year went on Mom noticed that she was sharing less and less of what she was earning. Raquel was trying to keep up with the other girls in her school, all of whom had more than three dresses and one pair of school shoes. It was sad to watch my mother and sister fight over money. My mother didn't understand the social pressures my sister was under, while my sister didn't understand the economic pressures my mother faced, even when working multiple jobs.

This was in the 1950s, but conditions today often require a family to work at least two jobs to pay the bills and feed their children. Poverty level income for a family of three like mine today is around $20,000 annually and even if you find a full-time job at the federal minimum wage of $7.25/ hour you only earn $15,000 a year, thus you are still under the poverty level income. That means that to feed your children, a family must work multiple jobs as my mother used to do, along with managing bus schedules, childcare between jobs and maybe doing side work late at night. I don't know how much my mother earned working at the car dealership but I knew that without that second job she couldn't pay all the bills at the end of the month. She wanted Raquel to help more on our household expenses and so they argued. I couldn't take sides.

Later in life when I ran the youth programs that Jerry Brown knew me from, I heard accounts of fights the teens in my programs had with their parents. We would almost always side with the young person, not trusting that their parents and guardians were making sacrifices or the right decisions. Even if it is seldom said explicitly, most professional social workers, even if just out of school, feel that they can make better decisions than low-income parents or guardians.

Also, it is difficult to get funding for social service programs unless you convince funders that families cannot solve their problems without the program. To get funding for my youth programs I had to imply that parents were disengaged, uncaring, or incapable. This was the presumption that my mother hated: the prevalent *deficit view* of her. To counter this tendency the *alternative* being presented starts by trusting parents until they prove otherwise. As a middle class parent, that is how I want to be treated.

Raquel and I were very close, though our personalities were very different. She was gregarious and social with a deep reservoir of sweetness. While I was quiet and uncomfortable in social situations, I found shelter in these two very strong, opinionated women.

Toward the end of the school year Raquel began sneaking out late at night. I would cover for her, pretending she was still in the bedroom we shared. Then one night she didn't come home. The next morning when my mother found out, she was in a panic. We called all Raquel's friends and found out that she had a boyfriend, an older Italian boy. That night my sister, who was sixteen at the time, brought her boyfriend, Chuck, to the house. We heard Raquel put her key in the door. My mother rushed towards the living room then stopped when she saw Chuck was there with Raquel. She was furious but she wasn't about to show it as they stood across from each other. I watched from the doorway of our bedroom, scared of what might happen.

Then Raquel dropped the bomb. She softly announced that she was pregnant, and then hurriedly declared that she and Chuck were going to get married and move away. My mother lost it and lunged at Chuck, but he was taller and stronger than her. Tears came to my eyes as I watched my mother plead with Raquel to stay in our home, but it didn't work. They soon left. My mother collapsed on the floor. I watched in anguish as my mother sobbed, wrenching with tears. Her daughter, my sister, my best friend, left our lives. That night my mother's cries were of the loss of hope. She had come to America to build a better life, not for herself, but for her two children. Now she had lost one of them.

For those inclined to depict my Mom as an uneducated, uncaring Mexican single parent, losing my sister in this way would be seen as further evidence. Some of Raquel's rich friends also got in trouble, but the more privileged weren't likely to experience the same harsh judgment. My mother put both of us in what were considered "good" schools but there were unanticipated consequences. It would have helped if my mother could have developed the business she wanted so that she didn't need to work two outside jobs. She tried to expand her dress making business, but there was nobody to help capitalize her, no investment system available to provide a boost to her tremendous talents.

After Chuck and Raquel left our apartment that night my mother tried to keep tabs on my sister. She didn't talk as much now but I could see and feel the pain in her heart. I carried the same sadness. My mother tried to find distractions for me including promising we would save money to go to Disneyland. But as with most children, my happiness was tied to hers. If there had been a way to make her happier or less stressed, then as her child I would have been happier.

Finally, one night after dinner, before I started washing dishes, and she started the ironing, she pulled me aside, leaned down, pointed her index finger and ordered with ferocious intensity:

"Mauricio, this is not *going to happen again. Promise me to go to college and not let things like this ever happen again!"* For the next eight years she met her part of the bargain, saving money, taking me to Disneyland, and getting me into and through the University of California at Berkeley. For me, her words are the challenge that I'm still trying to live up to.

CHAPTER TWO

No Welfare Queens
Unsticking the myth that families are "stuck"

For the next eight years my mother sacrificed everything to help Raquel, but also make sure that I would not end up in a bad situation and that I go to college. Chuck moved my sister to Syracuse New York, separating her and their three children from our family. He was insecure and volatile, refusing to let Raquel finish high school, or take a job that paid more than his own. He kept coming up with get-rich schemes and when they failed he took it out on Raquel, often beating her. During their worst times, Raquel would try to run away, and even attempted suicide. When she would run away with the kids, she, like most families in crisis, would need immediate charity and welfare. The welfare system and private charity act as safety nets; catching people in crisis, assessing their problems and needs, stopping their fall, and helping them to stabilize.

In the first few days of a crisis she had "tunnel vision" and was not in shape to make good decisions. I point this out because in chapter six it will be discussed how some studies, regarding those in crisis, use that immediate stage of confusion to promote it as a more permanent mental condition; that those like my sister can no longer make good decisions. They use studies of what is called toxic or chronic stress to advance the need for programs, not parents, to lead the change out of poverty. Yet what I observed is that within a couple days or weeks Raquel would stabilize and was fully able to plan and lead the change she wanted. She was smart and would find work because she was a hard worker, very organized, personable and talented. But as soon as she began to earn, usually starting at very low wages, her government benefits were cut. When she failed to earn enough to house and feed her kids, she was forced to return either to welfare or Chuck, who promised to never hit her again. She would have led her own change if there had been an *alternative* that provided a choice of benefits for the positive initiative she took to build an independent life.

It is a story that plays out today for abused parents who are trying to be responsible and who seek an safety and independence. If a minimum wage job only earns you $15,000 annually, after paying rent you may only have $5,000 for the rest of the year to feed and clothe your kids as well as travel to work. Just as it had been for us when my mother was working in the evenings, Raquel would need to leave her three kids at night to work a second job and the cost of childcare would likely cost most of what she would earn. Given very limited choices my sister made the best decisions she could.

Here's what I've learned from my sister's experience and my work in social service nonprofits: people truly need the welfare system when they are in a crisis. But we need a totally different and separate approach if we want people to build full, independent lives. What is being proposed is to create a *separate* benefit system that is similar to how we help the rich and privileged to get ahead. Once she was stable and working hard, Raquel needed an *alternative* to welfare or charity. Like my mother, she wanted to be a part of the incentive and benefits system our society makes available to the rich: tax breaks, investments, scholarships, awards, low-interest loans and preferential treatment. Charity, based on weaknesses, continues the deficit view and the disrespect the recipients feel. The rich don't feel disrespected when they take advantage of tax deductions, low interest rates or other preferential benefits. They feel they earn those privileges because they "contribute" to society. They feel entitled to benefits. But they are not the only ones that contribute and are entitled to benefits.

The national research group, CFED, studied the range of benefits government makes available and found that "The biggest beneficiaries of asset-building policies are those households who need the least help in saving and investing. Meanwhile, low-income families who could use the most help and even solidly middle-income families, receive a very low level of benefits from government policies." If we want a level playing field, if we want equal opportunity for all, we need to restructure our asset building benefits.

It's a myth that families living under the poverty level income are stuck and thus *not* contributing to society. Experts tell us that the poor are stuck in poverty and so investing in their efforts, as we invest in the rich, is not productive. But that lack of productivity was not my experience growing up. I saw my family and families like mine getting themselves jobs, even creating jobs. They paid taxes and helped elderly or disabled neighbors. But they earned so little that even an unexpected medical bill could send them back into poverty. Families like mine cycled back and forth in and out of poverty. Though my mother never told me her income, I could tell when we were living below the poverty line: when my mother didn't eat at dinner time and was most stressed, I knew that her hours had been cut or she was laid-off.

At times, she left a job when she faced a racist or sexist intolerable work environment. She was very pretty and her bosses felt their positions entitled them to come on to her. Being harassed by someone in a more powerful position than you is frustrating, but the humiliation cuts deeper than that.

"He's seeing how far he can go and then will blame it on my being pretty" is how she described those situations. Then one day I would hear,

"He touched me today" in a disgusted tone and I knew it was the end of that job. She would try to get better and better jobs but some work environments were intolerable. Facing harassment undermines the spirit. It had happened before so by telling me that he touched her my mother was warning me that food might be scarce in the near future. I knew she couldn't tolerate this treatment but she had to tolerate him for a while to get a decent recommendation for the next job. And that was the worst period for us. Every night I would see her feeling defeated even though she was doing her job well. She had to be nice to him because she needed a recommendation letter if she was to get another job at the same pay level. For a woman that wasn't coy, she had to play coy, then come up with an excuse about having to quit that he would believe so she could get the letter she needed. It was an awful period for her and for me because I could feel her pain and her shame each night.

She would quit as soon as she could and eventually she'd get another job, more hours, or more money from side sewing projects and we would be happy. I remember those times because our reward was to go to "Tad's Steak House" to get a cheap steak, baked potato, and garlic bread. Over dinner she would joke that if her car had broken down in Mexico, as she drove across the border so that I would be born in an American hospital, I would probably have ended up a waiter in Mexico! "But you are going to college, right?" she would always demand with a caring smile.

But between these cheap steak dinners at Tad's, there were plenty of times when the car did break down or she got sick; those would be the times we would barely have enough to eat. For that period of time we were counted as part of those "in poverty", but it was a temporary circumstance. In the face of every crisis or setback my mother kept going until we could afford that steak. She never gave up. She and our friends were all part of the vast majority of the poor that get themselves jobs, pay rent and taxes in spite of the racism, sexism or other prejudices they endure.

When I hear the term "generational poverty" today, I am skeptical. This overused phrase implies that once in poverty people stop trying and stay there for generations sucking up government benefits and social service programs. That wasn't my experience with my family or our friends and neighbors. I had seen my sister and Chuck try time and again to "make it". At times they would do pretty well and Chuck would be calm. But with few cushions to buffer a crisis, something always went wrong and they would fall back into poverty — and my sister bore the brunt of Chuck's frustrations.

Most of our neighbors were in the same situation: income fluctuated when someone got sick, a car broke down, they were harassed or hours were cut. Yet everyone persevered, picking themselves up after each crisis. Mostly we helped each other through those periods. Few people we knew had applied for welfare and if they did they used it as a transition and were off within a year, two at the most.

I therefore wondered where all of the "welfare queens" that I kept hearing about lived. If millions of people were not working and relaxing on welfare, where were they living? Not in the neighborhoods I knew and not in the neighborhoods I now work in. My mother moved us a lot and in every neighborhood that we lived in, people worked and worked *hard*. They just weren't paid very much.

The poverty that I experienced in my childhood was *episodic* poverty. It was when my mother lost a job or had her hours cut. My neighbors were maids, landscapers, security guards and some did seasonal work picking our food in California's Central Valley. Their income went up and down but it wasn't that they didn't work or didn't know how to work hard. Few were dependent on government benefits. The idea of "generational poverty" always seemed suspect to me.

In 2009 I finally found a series of census bureau studies[8] referred to earlier in the book — data from 2005 through 2014 — that confirmed my experience growing up in poor neighborhoods. All the studies found that chronic poverty was rare.

"Census Bureau Survey Shows Poverty is Primarily a Temporary Condition" was the headline of the press release in March of 2011. We regularly hear of the huge numbers of people "stuck" in poverty, generally 14 to 18 percent of our population, but what did the census bureau find? Between 2005 and 2007 only 3 percent continued in poverty after those

---

8   See Notes for the links to all the studies generally titled "Income and Poverty in the United States".

three years and between 2009 and 2012 only 2.7 percent continued living under the poverty line income. If half of those still in poverty at the end of each study have disabilities, are seniors, or face permanent issues that stop them from working, that likely means that only about 1.5 percent of our population could be remotely considered as welfare queens or "stuck". Reporting on these census studies in the Huffington Post, they noted:

> "There are people who need help briefly because they lost a job or something temporarily went wrong, and there are people who have longer-term circumstances — they have a disability or they're elderly, or they live in an economically isolated area like a rural town where a factory shut down."

This is far from the image that makes society think we have a lazy, passive underclass. But if this is true, why does the percentage of those in poverty stay at that 14 to 18 percent level year after year? The same census studies also document that within three years about 30 percent of those that had worked their way out of poverty temporarily fall back under the poverty income level, probably from the types of crises — like sickness or layoffs — that my family and our neighbors experienced. A similar study by the Urban Institute reports that 50 percent of the working poor fall *temporarily* below the poverty line within five years and we also know that some of our middle class falls into episodic poverty after a layoff and until they find a new job. In short, the up to 18 percent who we hear are in poverty are an ever-changing group of families, not one group of families that are "stuck". The average stay in poverty is around six months, not generations.

The following chart shows the spread of the population in the United States by income. It's clear that the vast majority of our population hovers around the poverty level, churning back and forth.

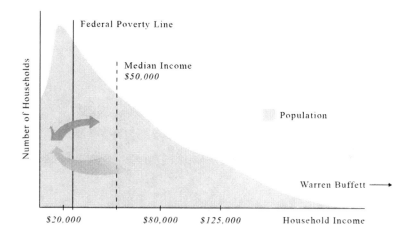

So, what happens once families work their way out of poverty? They enter the worst place to be in our economy. They become part of the working poor or lower middle-class who are ignored by our benefit and incentive policies noted by CFED above. We only offer them "charity".

The solid vertical line is the poverty level for a family of three. The dashed vertical line, median income, indicates that half of our population is to the left of that line and half is spread to the right. Warren Buffet and a few others of the very rich are way off to the right. The circular lines illustrate the episodic nature of being in poverty, more clearly shown on the next page.

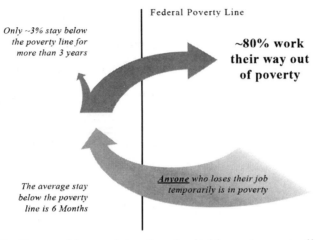

Sadly, as with my sister, the charitable system actually becomes just another barrier for low-income families to overcome when they begin to strive.

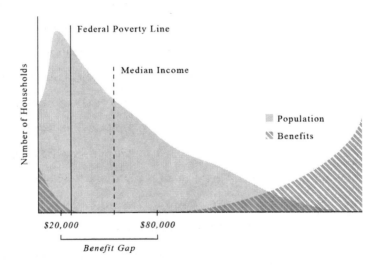

The chart above more roughly illustrates the benefits we make available to people. The dashed shaded area on the left depicts welfare and other benefits that are based on need. The less money you have, the more benefits you qualify for since the original intent of a means-tested system — measuring the extent of need — is to stabilize those in dire straits. That's not a bad thing. It is a safety net designed to catch people before they fall into abject poverty. My sister needed it when she fled her husband to protect herself and her children. The problem with the safety net is that when she took initiative and found employment, or saved money, those benefits were cut. Most welfare benefits are gone if your income goes above 120 percent of the poverty level.

The dashed shaded area on the right roughly depicts the benefits our country makes available to the well-off through mortgage interest deductions, tax breaks, etc. These benefits can total into the *millions of dollars* for the rich and benefits increase as people improve their wealth. But if you look closely at the studies you find that there are almost no benefits available once you get above the poverty line and not much is available until you make over $80,000 annually. These are just the obvious benefits — there are myriad of laws and loopholes to build wealth if you have wealth. It appears that Donald Trump might have been able to claim a loss of almost $1 billion because of real estate law loop holes and he could use that one loss to offset paying any taxes for 18 years. Clearly the working poor, as well as most of our middle class, are not eligible for such benefits. Additionally, if their businesses would have lost just a fraction of what his ventures lost they would have been judged as incompetent.

Given what the census studies have shown, the next time you see the story that reads that there are "45 million people stuck in poverty", question the word "stuck". Along with the phrases "generational poverty," the "culture of poverty," and "welfare queens," "stuck in poverty" falsely stigmatizes all the working poor, evoking images of helplessness or laziness and ignoring the vast majority of families who are working.

Researchers and journalists use these phrases recklessly, and incorrectly. A more accurate depiction of the working poor would bear witness to the hard work of those who clean our hotel rooms and wash our dishes, and the fact that those in poverty will only be there temporarily. The experts should report that the problem is not getting people above poverty, since all but a few percent climb out on their own, but that the *greatest challenge lies above the poverty line*, as part of the working poor. They enter the *benefit gap* shown in the previous chart. The United States has very few benefits for those that strive, even though they are facing prejudice and paternalism. If we feel we must incent the rich, then we must also ensure that working hard in America pays off for low-income families, helping them to also achieve success. If investing in the rich will grow our economy, then investing in the poor will do the same.

It's not possible to escape poverty through welfare since benefits are reduced as your income goes up and almost disappear if you earn more than poverty level income. That means that almost everyone who can work does work. Moreover, since one minimum wage job is not enough to get a family above the poverty line — and the census shows staying in poverty is temporary — it means that most people or families are working more than one job. *Laziness is as rare as decent pay*

For those caught in this churn, our current benefit system actually becomes a barrier to progress.

Margaret, a mother of three, has a special needs child, Ruben, and because she was on welfare he qualified for a subsidized special care program that was a perfect fit for him. Yet she wanted to get off welfare and began to work. She was taking control over her life and feeling very good about it. But when Ruben's wonderful program discovered that her income had gone above their eligibility income, he was immediately dropped from the program. Even with her new job, Margaret didn't earn enough to enroll him in a comparable private program. Her choices were stark: either quit her job immediately and get back on welfare if she wanted to keep him in the program where he thrived, or find another way to build a future for her family that didn't include welfare — or his program. Concluding that there would never be a future for her and her other children if she went backwards, she kept her job and found friends to care for Ruben. It was not as beneficial for Ruben, so she began organizing other families facing similar circumstances to help change the rules.

Looking back on those eight years that my mother struggled so hard to at least have one of her children succeed, it reminds me of how much determination it takes to live on poverty wages, face discrimination, harassment and know things will go wrong anyway because your options are so limited. Our society stereotypes and distrusts parents who lose a kid into a bad situation or fall back into poverty as a result of a crisis. Unfortunately, there are those on both the political left and right that assume that economically struggling parents are fundamentally flawed. That their plight is their fault. Yet, if there were an *alternative* set of benefits that could have recognized and invested in my mother's or sister's talents and hard work, our family history might have been different and both of her children may have prospered and contributed more to society as she dreamed.

CHAPTER THREE

Privilege and its Opposite
Berkeley, a bizarre out of body experience

The disparity in finances is only part of the difference between being poor and being well-off. Until I attended the University of California at Berkeley I didn't realize how different the world of the privileged is from the world in which I was raised. Today there is talk of providing low-income families with *equal opportunity*, but the opportunities I found in this privileged new world can't be replicated. Although it's unlikely that a truly level playing field can ever be created, the resourcefulness you learn when living without privilege — or money — can at least get you into the game and that ability should be respected.

There is a built-in advantage enjoyed by people who are raised in a world where they don't have to constantly worry about money. The privileged have access to choices and networks of support and opportunity I hadn't imagined. I was about to see this strange new privileged world firsthand.

Following my mother's directive to go to college, I tried to do my best in high school, but I wasn't a straight "A" student. My mother told me I had to become an engineer or a doctor; they made money and she needed to know that I could take care of myself, and my sister too. I was sure that if I became a doctor people would die, so I chose engineering hoping fewer would die from my work. Actually, I didn't have a clue as to what engineers did. In that period, there was no tuition at any of the University of California schools so I applied to each campus that had an engineering department. If the university had been charging tuition I wouldn't have even applied, just as its current tuition of about $13,000 annually for U.C. Berkeley means that many of today's young people don't apply.

I was in my senior year in high school, C. K. McClatchy High in Sacramento, California. Every day after school I would go to our mailbox anxiously awaiting a college acceptance or rejection letter. Then finally there it was, a letter from the University of California. The typeface seemed so elegant, as though it was from a different world.[9] I just stood there at the mailbox holding the letter, staring at the envelope and that elegant typeface.

I was overcome with fear. Everything had been sacrificed for me, for this moment, but what if I didn't get in? I felt I was suffocating in my house so I went and sat down on the street curb, my feet in the gutter, still just staring at the sealed envelope. It was a warm Sacramento day but the air felt stagnant, the sun brooding. There was only silence. No cars passed by. That nothing felt good only added to my fear. I was preparing myself

---

9   I still have that letter and I'm still fascinated by the elegant typeface.

for the worst. What would I tell my sister and my mother when they came home? I wondered if I should wait until someone was home so we could cry together. I hadn't applied to any "safe schools"[10] since we didn't know that was a normal strategy and my high school counselor had been no help.

The ten minutes I sat there seemed like hours until I finally got the courage to open the letter. I unfolded it and it began "Dear Mr. Miller: I am pleased to inform you ...." and I didn't finish the rest of the sentence. I was so relieved. I didn't care that I got into Berkeley, I just didn't want to disappoint my sister and mother. *Such is love.*

*

My first day on campus was a bizarre out-of-body experience. The whole four years were bizarre, but that first day was particularly surreal. My mother, with all my stuff piled in the back seat, drove me to Berkeley from Sacramento. I had never visited the campus. We didn't know that was what people did.

It was a beautiful August day and as we drove up to the curve in front of my dormitory I saw tons of kids hauling stuff out of their cars. Then as I opened the car door and stepped out bells began chiming a beautiful melody. For a split-second I wondered if the bells sounded just for me! I later learned that there is a bell tower on campus, the Campanile, and the chimes always play at noon. I had clearly arrived in a new world full of energy and opportunity. For a kid that had rarely left his neighborhood it was a bit like entering heaven, both exhilarating and terrifying.

After my mother left me, I went to my new room at Ehrman Hall off

---

10   By the time my kids were applying to colleges I had learned that they needed to apply to some "safe" schools where their grades could safely qualify them for entrance.

College Avenue, near campus. Watching everyone settle into their rooms was exciting — but it felt uncomfortable. This new world was one of assumed entitlement and privilege like I had never experienced. It didn't help that my assigned roommate, Gunar, walked in wearing a suit and tie. I didn't have a suit and tie! Fear swelled. Was there a dress code at U.C. Berkeley no one told us about?

Education is, of course, one of the strategies our country employs to create upward mobility. But while there are programs to help kids from poor families get into college, there are few ways to help them survive once admitted. Most programs do not address the stress that young people like me face because these two groups, the privileged and the working poor, occupy worlds that are so very different. Now, after decades of touting the benefits of education, researchers have noticed that the low-income kids that have been helped into colleges are graduating at a much lower rate than those from upper income families, even if the data is adjusted for abilities. Their reasons for dropping out of college ranged from a feeling of being isolated, not belonging, to the constant financial strain. As a story in the *Washington Post* put it, "[T]he afflictions of poverty don't just disappear after a student gets into college".

The world I left, that of my sister and mother, was a world of stress, insecurity, and anxiousness. That is what I remember the most about being poor. It wasn't about scarcity — not having food, or shoes — but the lack of control, the fear of what crisis the next day might bring. Charities were there to offer us food or clothes, and social programs tried to shape our decisions, but no one offered us the means to take control over our lives. Being a part of the low-income families that were constantly working to get, and stay, above the poverty line didn't erase the constant helpless feeling I had in my gut, or my desire to hide from that unstable reality. My family and I were always walking around knowing that life was not under control, and it took money to have the real choices we needed. We hoped the next calamity would not hit us, at least not yet. But we always knew it was coming.

Here, on campus, people didn't walk around that way. Everyone on my floor of the dormitory was cheery, at ease in the world. They seemed to be living a different reality. Gunar had a car and so did all my friends. Well, LeRoy had a motorcycle. But the biggest difference wasn't that they possessed material things that I didn't have. It was that they saw life in such a different way. They envisioned their future with a self-assurance that I didn't have. I was in college hoping — it was only a hope — that I would someday have a job that paid more than what my mother made. I didn't know that joining this new world would bring me so many privileges, or offer me automatic respect.

That sense of being respected was what was missing ever since the sixth grade when I was walking up the school stairs and a big kid walking down the same side slapped the books out of my hands and shoved his way past me yelling, "Get out of the way chink!" He said it with such disdain that I stood frozen. My mind swirled. He didn't know me and yet he hated me? Because I looked somewhat Asian? How could that be? What could I do? I would have handled it better if he called me a dirty spic. I was Mexican and proud of that. I could have emotionally coped with a slur against Mexicans because my mother had prepared me for that. But a chink? I had no defense. And the fact that none of the dozens of other kids on the stairs who heard the slur stopped to help me pick up my books made me wonder if all of them looked down on me too. I think I resented the onlookers more than the one who yelled at me. By not helping me they accepted that racist act. I wondered; did ninety percent of the other kids that saw this slur also look down on me, or did only ten percent of the bystanders hate me for looking different?

That one racist incident crushed my self-confidence outside of my closest circle of friends. Later, it limited the women I was willing to ask out on dates. I remember overhearing a guy asking someone out and her reply was "Hell would freeze over before I would go on a date with you!" I didn't know if she said that because he was a jerk or because he was Mexican, but I wasn't going to take the chance.

I knew this happened to the black kids more and wondered how they coped. I couldn't let myself indulge in self-pity. I chose instead to feel admiration for all those who persevered in the face of racism like my mother who secretly clung to her pride in being a strong woman, as well as being Mexican, as the way to emotionally handle the prejudice she faced. Those in the social sector should not underestimate the negative impact that society's prejudices have on those it wants to help, but rather than show pity there should be a show of admiration. If we want a more level playing field we have to address the stereotypes and bigotry that pits us one against the other. Society would fare much better if we admired and respected one another.

In my freshman year at U.C. Berkeley there were very few kids from low-income neighborhoods that I could relate to. I was surprised by how confident my classmates were. They seem to have grown up expecting to have choices and control over their lives. They didn't *hope* they could get jobs, they *expected* to get jobs. Their only concern was to find a type of work they wanted in the type of firm they wanted. In my family, we didn't expect to have choices. Our talents were ignored out of necessity. I declared engineering as my major because my mother told me to and I owed her that. My friends talked about taking different classes to discover their talents and what they wanted to do. It was news to me that you could be in college for two years before you had to declare a major.

I came to learn that the difference between these two worlds was not just a lack of money or material things. The real difference was in the expectations about how to deal with power structures and the belief in how you could shape your future. I was sent to college to get a good job. For my roommates and friends, college was a reinforcement of their power and the control they expected to have over their future. Higher education was something they grew up feeling entitled to. They assumed that our nation's systems, institutions, and even governing bodies, were supposed to cater to them. This entitlement, even by kids my age, became much clearer about a month into my freshman year with the start of the Free Speech Movement, FSM, at U.C. Berkeley.

The power of many

My experience at Berkeley during the crazy years of 1960s activism also taught me that when faced with structures more powerful or privileged than you, collective action can level the playing field.

On October 2nd, 1964, someone yelled down the hallway of my dorm floor that there was a protest going on in Sproul Plaza, the large open area in front of the U.C. administration building on campus. I quickly put on my tennis shoes — new for college — and headed to Bancroft Avenue, the main street fronting the campus. As I walked towards the plaza I saw

44

a line of police cars and police motorcycles parked along the street. As I passed the alley behind the administration building, I saw dozens of policemen in full riot gear assembled in military order, standing shoulder to shoulder, awaiting orders.

Both my pace and pulse quickened as I headed to Sproul Plaza. When I turned into the plaza I got my first view of the protest. My heart and mind exploded. In front of me thousands of students — yes thousands — were sitting on the ground completely surrounding one police car on the plaza. I was told there was a student inside the car who the police had tried to arrest. Another young man was standing on the roof of the police car with a bullhorn yelling about freedom of speech. "My God," I thought with excitement, "so this is college?!!" I learned that it was Mario Savio, later to become a leader of the Free Speech Movement[11], on top of that police car with the bullhorn.

I'd grown up in poor neighborhoods where the police were less than friendly. I wondered why the policeman leaning against the car did not seem upset with the student above him denting the cruiser's roof? Where I was from if you dented a police car the officers wouldn't be so nice. But, of course, it helped that there were about 3,000 students sitting around the car. One individual did not hold the power in this situation. Power came from the collective action. It made sense to me. I thought, "America extolls individuality but if you aren't rich and well connected, then power comes from collective action, whether it is two people or 3,000 rebellious students."

Eventually the administration and students came to an agreement and

---

11   The Free Speech Movement (FSM) was a large student protest that took place in the 1964-65 academic year on the University of California, Berkeley campus. The protests wanted the administration to lift the ban of on-campus political activities and acknowledge the students' right to free speech and academic freedom.

the police car was finally able to drive off. The student in the car and the others were not charged for this incident. This was the start of dozens of student-led movements from free speech to the sexual freedom movement. There were the Brown Pride, Black Pride, and Yellow Pride movements for the Hispanic, Black, and Asian communities — Asians weren't yet considered the model minority. At that time in our history it was clear that pride in self and community was the cornerstone for change — something my mother extolled. Charity doesn't instill pride and programs led by professionals don't instill pride or self-confidence.

Of the activism I saw, I was particularly taken by the Black Pride movement[12] and the ways men and women self-organized and took care of one another. Just as the black community came together after slavery and, against all odds, built entire towns, the civil rights movement ultimately framed what had been thousands of small self-organized local actions into a national movement. Having grown up with only female role models, I looked for male role models, and I was particularly taken by the leadership of men in the emerging movements for freedom and civil rights. I especially admired the Black Panthers.[13] The Panthers would not allow blacks in their community to panhandle, just as my mother would scold any Mexican panhandling, but instead pressed them to join their movement where all were fed. Pride in community was everyone's responsibility. The men and women in that movement started food and housing programs for their

---

12   The Black Pride movement encouraged the celebration of black culture and African heritage. There were similar though not as significant Asian Pride and Brown Pride movements. The Black Pride movement led to other related movements such as the black power, black nationalism and the Black Panthers.

13   The Black Panther party, BPP, was active in the United States from 1966 until 1982. Besides acting as protectors in their neighborhoods they began health clinics and food programs. But FBI Director J. Edgar Hoover called their expansion "the greatest threat to the internal security of the country" and he led an extensive program to undermine the Panther leaders and members.

families. They even started their own schools. Fifty years ago these self-help efforts built a strong sense of community pride and mutuality and became the foundation for change. Now this mutuality is the exception. So, what happened?

The Black Panthers may have answered that back in 1966 at a rally on campus. One of my roommates yelled out, "The Panthers are going to march to Sproul Plaza". Since most of the Panthers were not students they weren't supposed to come on campus, but that was the point — to challenge the administration and the power structure. They had come to speak about President Johnson's emerging War on poverty.[14]

Most of us assumed that they were going to praise the President's effort. But the Panthers understood society better than I did at that point. I watched as they marched onto campus, police watching them carefully. There were only seven of them, all in black jackets with berets, each carrying a rifle. They explained that the weapons were to protect themselves and their community from the "pigs", the police. They then went on to explain all the work they intended to do for their community from housing to education. They wanted the control and the responsibility that comes with that initiative. Then their speech turned to Johnson's proposed war on poverty.

Most of the students with me were there to support the Panthers but they confronted us instead. "This war on poverty? Hell, it is only going to create jobs for you guys" they yelled, pointing to those of us in the audience. "We want to solve our own problems but all the money will go to you. You are all going to end up as poverty pimps making a living as

---

14   The War on Poverty was introduced by President Lyndon B. Johnson at his 1964 State of the Union address. It sought to expand the role of the federal government in reducing poverty levels.

long as we don't have anything!" That was the first time I ever heard the term "poverty pimp" but I understood the meaning. Maybe Jerry Brown was also at that rally. The applause was mixed from the student audience and then the Panthers marched off campus, again closely monitored by the campus police.

Were the Panthers right about the War on poverty? As decades passed and I saw anti-poverty programs proliferate, I saw how programs usurped the authority of struggling parents — they certainly replaced the self-help efforts started by the Panthers. In a 2013 article titled the "Charitable Industrial Complex" in the New York Times, Peter Buffet, son of Warren Buffet, wrote that "Between 2001 and 2011, the number of nonprofits increased 25 percent. Their growth rate now exceeds that of both the business and government sectors. It's a massive business with approximately $316 billion given away in 2012 in the United States alone, and more than 9.4 million employed." Others have called the nonprofit sector a playground for the well-intended.

Social status and its privileges

Many of my fellow students felt that the Civil Rights Act and other policy changes would level the playing field. Unfortunately, laws and policies do little to address the underlying privilege that social class and status provides informally. Privilege frees people to dream and the strong social networks available to the privileged allows them to make their dreams a reality. I was in Berkeley to get a job, not dream, but I quickly began to learn about how those that inhabited the world of privilege use their social status and networks.

Some of my engineering student friends designed what we called the "machine" that could be used to break into most any room on our campus and more to the point, most rooms on the Stanford campus, our rival college. I built my own machine and practiced breaking into my room. The first time I went on a raid using my machine, we went to steal pure alcohol, ethanol, out of the chemistry lab to bring to a party. As it should be for one's first heist, it was a dark and blustery night. Very few people were in the chemistry building and the lab door was locked. However, I knew the room and that the door could be opened by turning the inside door knob.

Our machine was made of two straightened coat hangers strung together so it could slide under the door. Both ends of the coat wire were bent 90 degrees and off one of ends a piece of scotch tape dangled from the bent section. A string was attached to the other end of the tape. We slid the end of the wire with the tape and string under the door. Then from our end of the hanger wire we twisted it up vertically and because the height of the bend was adjusted to be just above the door knob, we rotated the wire so it swung and left the tape sticking over the inside knob. When we gently pulled the string, the tape then turned the inside knob. Magic. The door opened and we got our ethanol.

Breaking into places and stealing was not like me but this was my second year at college and I had seen that every time my college friends got caught doing "pranks" they were let off with a warning. The police and administrators looked on it as youthful creative fun. If a kid had done this in my neighborhood, also for fun, they would have had the book thrown at them. In 2014, the shooting of Michael Brown in Ferguson, Missouri, was argued to be partly justified because he allegedly stole cigarettes from a convenience store, something my college friends did all the time. Such are the differences of social status in the United States.

These were my first lessons about the privilege of social status. Race, of course, also plays a significant role but it was clear that the college kid is not only given the benefit of the doubt by the police, but more than that, in that same year, I began to learn how those that are middle/upper income use their social networks to gain other benefits.

There was a lot of partying going on during the school year, especially at the fraternities. I rarely went to these parties but some of the guys on our floor went to a frat party one night, got in a fight, and were arrested. "Good", I thought, "there *are* limits!" But then I learned that it helps to know someone that knows someone that can pull strings or apply pressure. "My father knows a lawyer that knows the mayor," or something of the sort would be said when anyone got in trouble. Sure enough, the kids arrested were let out in less than 24 hours. I didn't know how that would work for me; if I called my mother under similar circumstances I would still be in jail. There seemed to be a set of rules that I knew I couldn't access, although now that I'm middle income I totally know that social networks are where the power lies.

Of course, social connections can do more than get you out of jail. Over eighty percent of jobs are filled through social network contacts. My friends encouraged me to go to parties and make more friends who might be well connected. For an introvert like me, this was hard. But my mother was more attuned to the power of connection because that was also the way things worked in Mexico. My first decent summer job came about because my mother shared with her boss that I was in college to be an engineer. He then connected me to a summer internship with Union Carbide Corporation. Summer jobs had always been so difficult for me to get but that year I learned that the managers' kids always got great summer positions, often without even being interviewed. And just as my friends predicted, after graduation the best job offer I got was from Union Carbide Corporation where I had spent the summer. My friends took their networking access for granted, without realizing they enjoyed a tremendous advantage over those from my background. Some of their fathers would talk about how they made it totally on their own initiative, how they "bootstrapped" it. They didn't seem to realize they lived in a world that automatically gave them advantages.

So how do we develop a level playing field and equal opportunities when so many benefits are already confined within the social networks of the few? The privileged and well-networked get first shot at everything.

What if there are new tools that can begin to bridge that privilege gap? I think technology can help. Expanding peoples access to the internet and digital technology can present a bridge, even if limited in scope. On social networking sites people can't see how rich or poor you really are. You can reach across class and racial lines. You can crowd source solutions. Even if you only have a smart phone you can do research and access the same information as anyone else. My mother could have used technology to display her dress designs and maybe get investors, sales. Students from any background can demonstrate their talents, share their stories and connect with new social networks to get better opportunities. We see immigrant and refugee families staying connected with relatives in their home country through the internet. Soldiers serving overseas share "face time" with their children at home. Phones and mobile apps connect us all and can bring us closer together, rather than farther apart. Technology is a significant tool for the *alternative*.

CHAPTER FOUR

The Ultimate Sacrifice
'Inspiring revolution with a chicken and two potatoes'

After graduating from Berkeley in 1968, I took a job as a plant engineer with Union Carbide Corporation at their Pittsburgh, California plant. I could finally send money home. Less than a year later in early 1969, my career as an engineer was interrupted when I was drafted[15] and sent to the war in Vietnam. I was the only Berkeley graduate I knew that ended up serving. There were a number of ways to get out of the draft, but most took money or connections. Some of my friends turned to lawyers, some had enough money to go to graduate school, and some without responsibilities at home, left for Canada. None of those actions were options for me. My mother was becoming ill and even in the Army I had to send

---

15 In 1969 the draft changed to a lottery system. If you got a high number there was a lower chance of being drafted. My bad luck was that the lottery started 2 months after I was ordered to report for service. I never tried to find out what my lottery number might have been. It was depressing enough that I got drafted on my birthday.

money home to help her and my sister. Our family was drained.

My mother was sure I would die in Vietnam and that both of her kids would be lost before achieving the dreams she'd had for us. She began to hate America and our journey here. At one point she stopped writing to me. Later, I asked her why. "I dreamt you had died and I didn't want to live," she answered. But I survived the war and came back determined to help my family and to prove that America was worthy of our trust.

After being released from the Army in 1971, Union Carbide Corporation was obligated to give me my job back since I had been drafted out of it. Instead of giving me a job back in the Bay Area, however, they sent me to Ashtabula, Ohio just outside of Cleveland. It was 110 degrees when I left Vietnam and minus 5 with a chill factor of minus 35 when I stepped off the plane in Cleveland, Ohio a few weeks later. I resented the war, I resented authority, I resented the cold and resented the lack of control I had over my life. I was an angry young man but I was relieved to finally be sending more money home. I had been away from Raquel and Mom for three years.

Upon my return to the States I found that my mother's health had worsened over those years. There had been no universal healthcare system that she could turn to. The jobs my mother was able to get were unstable and the employers that paid more did not provide health benefits. Instead of going to doctors for her care, she saved for me and Raquel. These were the choices she made.

My mother wouldn't tell me all the details of her illnesses but I learned she had bleeding ulcers, needed an operation on her esophagus, and was suffering from intestinal troubles. Physically worn down by decades of hard work and stress, my mother suffered in silence. I knew that now it was my turn to take care of her. By this time, my sister had run away from Chuck and she found and married a wonderful man, Jim Roberts. She was safe, but her three children stayed with Chuck and their lives became troubled. Still, things had calmed down somewhat and my mother wanted me to pursue my interest in becoming a product designer.

Like my mother, I loved designing and making things. I wanted to use the G.I. Bill[16] educational benefits to get a master's degree in design, but I also wanted to take care of her. She and I argued. She didn't want the operations she needed and insisted that I move on with my life and forget "wasting your money on me." Once, we had a very heated argument. "Why did I give up my health?" She yelled, "Just to have you spend all your time taking care of me? You have to forget the past. Just forget!" She spoke as if she were the past. I pushed back that it was my turn to help her open the dress shop and get the RV she always dreamed about. That night, our arguments ended in a stalemate. But in the months ahead, as I planned to leave engineering, move back to Berkeley to study design and get her the medical care she needed, she stopped arguing. I thought I had won the argument.

My sense of victory hit a wall in the early hours of August 10, 1973. I was startled awake by a knock on the door. It was a bit past four in the morning. The night was dark except for the occasional headlights of the cars passing on Atlantic Boulevard, the main street of Alhambra, California. The knock came again, more forcefully, and I staggered toward the door.

"I'm coming. Who is it?" I hollered. "The police!" came the answer.

---

16 For those that served and were honorably discharged from military service the "G.I. bill" provided a small monthly stipend to offset the costs of attending an accredited college. This benefit still exists and is used by many who have served.

I opened the door and the policeman seemed to step back a little. The light hitting the porch was dim and he looked like a shadow. I couldn't see his face, but he didn't seem as anxious to talk to me as his knock had indicated.

"Yeah, what's happening?" I asked sleepily, thinking there was a neighborhood problem. "Are you Maurice Miller?" he asked. "Yes" I answered now realizing it wasn't about the neighborhood.

"Do you know a Bertha Miller?" My heart jumped to my throat and began to race. My whole body shivered. "Yes … she's my mother," I stammered. I didn't want to ask why he was asking. Maybe there was a different Bertha Miller they were looking for.

"I'm sorry to wake you, but we thought you would want to know." He hesitated a moment. "Your mother was found in a Las Vegas hotel." God, it *was* about my mother! How did he know that she had gone there for the weekend I wondered as a stream of thoughts raced through my mind.

"We believe she shot herself … in her room. Some of the hotel staff found her … I'm sorry… " His voice faded as my mind began to spin. I'm not sure what he said after the word "shot." I think I might have asked if she was dead.

Now I knew I had lost the argument. She had insisted that I not spend money on her. Two weeks before my putting a deposit down for an apartment for the two of us she stopped me. *My heart broke.*

*

I know that I am my mother's success in life — the most singular goal she was determined to achieve. She got me out of poverty in her own unique way. Yet in her struggle to save at least one of her two children she became tired, sick, and drained. Once she knew she had succeeded with me she was adamant that I move on. Going through her papers I found indications that she had developed her plan at least six months before that August day.

I rarely shared this story partly because too many of those that heard it assumed that my mother must have had some mental health problems. Yet almost any parent knows that they would die for their child. Society doesn't realize the extent to which low-income parents sacrifice for their children. Instead of being viewed as a bad mother or incapable of making good decisions, she should have been viewed as heroic. Still she couldn't shed the negative stereotype we overlay on the poor in life or in death.

Those at the bottom of our economy are dying and sacrificing every day and there is an urgent need for fundamental change, for a real paradigm shift. But the government and the philanthropic foundations I have known display no sense of urgency as they develop strategic plans on how to help those at the bottom of our economy. "The problem of poverty is complex" is the excuse I hear as they take their time developing elaborate theories and plans. Government and private philanthropy are good at talking and planning, but even after a fifty year war on poverty they never consider the possibility that their top-down solutions and plans will never solve poverty or create economic mobility.

People generally credit any professional success I've attained to my degrees from U.C. Berkeley. The truth is they were significant but not fundamental. Even now as I get awards, U.C. Berkeley uses them to promote itself and garner donations. That's not bad, but the truth is that all credit for my life should go to my mother and sister for the love, sacrifice, and resolve I relied on to make it through that crazy school. I felt alone at

Berkeley. I contemplated suicide while at Berkeley. That school almost killed me and certainly didn't love me. So who gets credit and respect? Who should we, as a society, acknowledge? Our society takes family and community for granted but it shouldn't. Family and the adults that keep communities together are fundamental and should be respected. If my mother and sister were recognized as the real key to my success, maybe instead of donating to a University, people would have invested in the business my mother wanted to start or in the career that my sister could have had.

Decades after losing my mother, credit is still being misdirected. On February 9th, 2011 at a conference, the Gathering of Leaders, convened by an FII funder, New Profit, I saw a wonderful spoken word performance by Daniel Beaty titled Dance Mama Dance. It went something like this:

I feel my mama's presence. So many things I never got to say. Mama, I saw you raise five of us by yourself with a father nowhere in sight. I saw you inspire revolution with a chicken and two potatoes. I saw you limp home late at night with sores on your feet. I saw you gracefully remove groceries from the cart when the bill got too high. I saw you pray when brother stole the microwave to buy drugs, ... I saw you hold a home together like a foundation that would never crumble, …but mama, I never saw you dance. I never saw you dance ……… So dance mama dance, break the flood gates of countless un-cried tears, …. Dance mama dance, for all the dreams that you forgot so we could make it through the day. Dance mama dance, like your nightmare is ending …

— and so goes the tribute that Daniel Beaty performed in honor of his mother. After this performance, Daniel, now an accomplished writer and performer, told the audience about the ups and downs of his childhood. He mentioned his early love for writing, recalling that in one school a teacher noticed his writing and sent his paper in to a contest that won him recognition. He continued writing and ultimately earned a scholarship to Harvard.

During the question and answer period members of an audience of funders, policy makers, and social service providers, asked, "So besides the school teacher that recognized your writing, what or who else really helped you?"

The next day I was leading a workshop at the conference. I asked those in my workshop who they saw as the most important influence in Daniel's life. "The school teacher of course," came the first response. When I asked who agreed, everyone in the room raised their hand. I was a little stunned by the unanimity, but not really surprised. Not one person answered "his mother."

It is the same when I tell people about my life. Often those on the outside of a situation look for the interventions made by institutions or outsiders. But this focus on external help diminishes the foundational relationships of family and close friends. Although Daniel had not only written a play in tribute to his mother and presented a beautiful, moving performance of his dreams for her in front of all of us, still no one recognized her importance in his life. This oversight contributes to, and is deeply rooted in our system's disdain for low-income families, primarily the parents and guardians. I'm sure that many people would have dismissed

Daniel's mother as another black single mom on welfare. Her color, her rag tag clothes, and the sight of her limping home would label her as a charity case at best. Which of us would really have suspended judgement to find and admire that she could inspire revolution with a chicken and two potatoes?

My mother's actions were unique, but I have seen other parents and guardians make amazing sacrifices and difficult choices for their children just as my mother and Daniel's mother did. Refugee parents endure dangerous treks to put their children into better situations. Parents without sufficient means miss meals and give up their personal dreams for their children. If needed, most parents and guardians will make a lifetime of sacrifices to create a better life for their children.

The emotional, unrecognized toll of not having sufficient choices to build one's future is much greater than the episodic loss of a meal or even the care of a doctor. Families seeking help from the social sector give up some of their dignity and self-respect in exchange for a free bag of groceries. But it is the loss of dignity and control over your own life that leads to the stress that my family endured and at times can't be endured by everyone; a small percentage of families turn to addiction or crumble under the weight and then are judged for their desperate acts.

Those that assume that my mother's final act was a result of depression or mental illness ignore the determination and heroic sacrifices she made for her children. We all have a choice as to how to view others across our socio-economic divide and that choice will determine the future of our country. Rather than assume the worst in people, we can combat the divisions that afflict us by celebrating each other's contributions and positive actions. We rarely see and celebrate the resilience and sacrifices of the many who strive every day, invisible as our receptionists, clerks, security guards, gardeners, or maids.

CHAPTER FIVE

A Race to the Bottom
Replacing the war on poverty with a dating service

On September 4, 1977, at 2:40 am, a group of young men, members of the Joe Boys gang in San Francisco's Chinatown, pushed their way through the front door of the Golden Dragon restaurant. Spotting members of the rival Wah Ching gang across the room, the Joe Boys pulled out their guns. Bullets began flying as onlookers jumped for cover. The battle was the Joe Boys' retaliation for the killing of Felix Huey by the Wah Ching earlier that year. When the shooting finally stopped, five people were dead and eleven others had been injured. Because two tourists were killed, the Golden Dragon massacre, as it became known, was the most publicized in a long history of San Francisco gang shootings.

After my mother's death I returned to U.C Berkeley to get a Master of Arts degree in design. I often ate at the Golden Dragon restaurant since it stayed open all night. I was very aware of the gang wars in San Francisco and the growing number of nonprofit organizations trying to address the underlying social problems in the poorest communities. With my mother's death still hanging over me, I wondered if instead of pursuing design I should join a nonprofit to see if families like mine could be helped.

My opportunity to join the nonprofit sector was precipitated by the Golden Dragon shootout. A group of my friends from U.C. Berkeley's architecture department started an organization called Asian Neighborhood Design, AND, which would offer local kids a way to leave gang life. My friends wanted to use their architectural skills to improve the offices of the many new nonprofits joining the war on poverty. They decided to recruit and train gang kids, who wanted out of a dangerous life, to work on the renovations of these new offices. My friends understood that that most kids joined gangs for protection and to experience the kind of security and respect not available to them as part of the bottom of our economy.

I was doing construction on the side to pay for college and was asked if I would lead the new construction-training program for gang members. I was hesitant; I was just finishing a Master's degree in design and had always dreamed of being a product designer. I was also mindful of the death of a youth worker named Barry Fong-Torres, a graduate of the Berkeley School of Criminology, who had also worked with gang kids. Fong-Torres was killed by gang members in his apartment on June 26, 1973, just as the gang wars were starting.

Although it sounded risky I had survived the Vietnam War and since my mother was no longer alive to tell me otherwise, I took the job. I was to train 25 gang-affiliated youth to work construction, and later help them find jobs. This was my first job in social services. I would soon learn that for all the good we did, there were some fundamental flaws in how the war on poverty was being waged

The first flaws - 1978 to 1981

Most of the money for the AND construction training program came from a government source called CETA, the Comprehensive Employment and Training Act. Like most social service funding, it required that we serve those classified as "most in need." The more we could show that our clients were needy or "at risk," the more competitive our program would be for funding. Recruiting gang members who wanted to leave the gangs wasn't easy. Although we weren't targeting the most entrenched and hardened gang members, we didn't directly approach other gang members either. Instead, we turned to their families and girlfriends who usually were pushing them to get out while they could — who we called "go-bees" for go-betweens. Gangs are social networks and a form of community. As in most communities word of mouth is the best reference. Once a few tough kids joined our program, word of mouth spread and I was able to fill most of the training slots.

I had only one training slot left to fill when two kids, Ben and Richard, stopped in to apply. Ben was taller than Richard, probably 5'8", slim and seemed more like a leader, coaxing Richard to come inside my office. Richard was not happy to be there and was scowling at Ben — he didn't meet my eyes at all.

We had kids from all over San Francisco in the program yet the gang rivalries did not seem to surface since all of these kids wanted out. The families of Ben and Richard lived in hotels with single rooms originally built to house the Chinese workers brought in to build the rail roads or other projects. They were mostly crowded small rooms that shared baths and kitchens with other residents. It seemed no wonder that the kids spent most of their time on the streets.

One of the go-bees helping us, Gloria, had told me that these friends might apply, and that Richard had just gotten out of jail for a burglary. He had tried and failed to get Ben to go on the heist with him. Although gang members are usually portrayed as scary and violent, Ben and Richard did not live up to the stereotype. They were both 17, had dropped out of school at 16 and before the robbery the worst crime either of them had committed was selling firecrackers illegally. Like so many others, they had joined the gang because it provided them some protection and elicited respect from others.

"We heard we could learn how to do carpentry and we want to apply," Ben declared, his tone demanding respect. Richard was timid, but when he cast his eyes toward me, his gaze was filled with challenge. I told them to sit down and gave them applications but then warned them that there was only one training slot left. Hearing that Richard sat up in his chair, wearing a half smile of relief. I reviewed their applications and saw that in terms of income, education, and other factors, the two were similar. But Richard had a criminal record for the burglary so I needed to consider him more at risk than Ben. My funding required we serve the "most in need" but I was torn as I looked over at the two of them sitting a few feet away from me at one of the long tables in the room. Here I was faced with Ben, a kid who was trying to do the right thing — who was trying to get training and hopefully set himself up for a good job — and a kid with a bad attitude who didn't want to be there. But the decision was not mine to make.

"I have to give the slot to Richard," I said. They both seemed startled and both looked questioningly at me. I felt a bit ashamed and defensive.

"Richard has a criminal record and is more in need," I added feeling my excuse was dumb and knowing that the eligibility requirements for my program used the wrong lens to look at these kids.

A bit startled but with an "I told you so" tone in his voice Richard turned to his pissed off friend.

"See," Richard gloated. "Looks like you shoulda' gone on that job with me after all!"

I got a sick feeling in my stomach. What kind of message had I just sent to a couple of teenagers? Ben looked disgusted, and I felt for him because he was like me. Growing up I had tried to stay out of trouble, but all of the help seemed reserved for those who did get in trouble. Ben slumped over, angry but still supportive of Richard. I could see it from both sides because my sister and her kids also made mistakes. I knew second chances after mistakes were vital. Yet for kids that hadn't made those mistakes, like Ben, few opportunities existed.

Opportunities were for the exceptional — the homeless kid smart enough to be at the top of the class at Harvard, or the kid overwhelmed with problems who becomes a program's success story. Being ordinary did not make you competitive for opportunities or services. People like Ben just didn't appear needy enough. Only a month into my first nonprofit job it was clear that unless there was an *alternative* that created opportunities for the Bens of the world, our current system of help, based on need alone, would continue sending the wrong message.

Replacing the war on poverty with a dating service

Richard was in my first training crew — twenty-four young men and one woman with gang ties. Richard was a really good person if you got past the tough exterior he used as a shield. He knew that staying in the gang was a dead end that might literally leave him dead. Though he worked hard in the program, given his creative interests, I doubted he was really cut out for construction. He liked design just as I did and if there had been choices, or he had money, he should have been in an art or design program.

The training program grew and so a second instructor, Dale, was hired. Almost as soon as Dale walked in the room I felt Richard grow tense. At the end of that first day I learned that Dale had been doing youth work previously and had a run in with Richard. Although they both seemed to be trying to keep the peace, one day they had an argument. As the director of the program I felt compelled to back Dale, my co-instructor, but when I did, Richard flew off the handle and with a "fuck you" aimed at me, he stormed out leaving his tool belt and hammer.

The following day Dale and I were apprehensive as the trainees came in. We didn't know what Richard's mood would be. About an hour after we started the training, someone came in to let us know that Richard was outside. I stepped outside to speak with him and found him standing partly in the street.

"I want my tool belt and tools!" he yelled at me.

"Can I talk with you?" I asked, and he only told me go fuck off. I went inside and retrieved his things while Dale listened from the inside, hidden behind the door. I handed Richard his tools and as he walked away he yelled back, "You tell that fucking liar that I'm going to kill his ass," and a few steps later he added, "and you too!" I stood frozen, not so much scared, as grieving. It was clear that Richard felt I had betrayed him. He had trusted me and I had betrayed that trust in order to do my job professionally.

The days and weeks after that confrontation in front of the training center were tense. Gloria was our eyes and ears. She told us Richard was seriously mad at Dale. Dale, remembering how Barry Fong-Torres had been shot because of a similar confrontation with a gang member, immediately quit. He actually moved to San Diego. As for me, I began carrying a weapon — just a knife — for the first time since leaving Vietnam. Gloria would call me now and again to reassure me. Richard was pissed at me but his fury was reserved for Dale.

Almost a year passed. I heard that Richard had a girlfriend, that he was getting his life together and that they were going to have a baby. As I was walking down Grant Avenue in Chinatown one day, Richard stepped out of one of the stores in front of me. We saw one another and unexpectedly, almost by reflex, we both smiled at the same time. I told him that I had heard he was doing really well and congratulated him on the baby. He just laughed and told me about his girlfriend, Marina, how she was his anchor. She had changed everything, he said. I must admit that I felt proud of him even if I hadn't been the one to help him.

For Richard, change came with that first date with Marina. His story wasn't the first I'd heard of a girlfriend being the key to change in a young man's life. I started thinking that maybe instead of running a training program we should be running a dating service. I was serious about this. So serious that I found and had a conversation with one of the managers of Great Expectations, the prominent dating service in the early 1980's. Fortunately, I was less than skilled in the matchmaking arena, so I dropped the idea. But I never shook the belief that personal loving relationships are far more transformative than social programs — and they cost a lot less, too. The *alternative* was going to have to bolster, not weaken, caring personal relationships.

Now that I was in the social network of other U.C. Berkeley graduates it was becoming clear to me that most of my opportunities were coming because of those relationships. My job at AND, for instance, was never advertised. It came because of those who knew me. Kids from my neighborhood never had a chance to apply. When I wanted an apartment, a dog, or even a good restaurant I would go to my network. I was learning more and more about how important it was to keep and expand social networks. But I also knew that nonprofit and government programs rarely focused on networking as a skill. They prioritized what they considered to be more tangible skills, like training to be a construction worker, above relationships and social networking.

At a conference, one of my funders had his teenage son sit next to me. For a high school student he was very polished as he asked me what I did and I asked him his interests in school. Then towards the end of the event he asked for my business card as he handed me his business card.

"You have business cards?" I asked somewhat puzzled by this teenager. "Yes" he replied. "It is part of the class requirements."

It appears that elite high schools teach networking!

In 1981, I became the executive director of AND, and soon I was confronted with the same contradiction I had faced in choosing Richard over Ben. The mother of a previous trainee, Joe Thompson, came to my office. It was around 3pm and Mrs. Thompson was stopping by between her day job as a lunch waitress and her evening job at a friend's beauty salon in her neighborhood. She was out of breath and in a hurry because our office was out of her way; she'd probably taken three buses to get to us.

"You remember Joseph, my son, went through your program last year," she said still catching her breath, "but you told my younger son Landon he couldn't get in. Why can't you take him?"

Joseph, a tall husky kid, had been a handful and because of that we thought his mom might be checked out or uncaring, yet here she was pleading for her son. She explained that so far, she had been successful in keeping her second son from joining a gang. She looked a bit desperate leaning toward me across my desk, her hands clenching the edge. She kept looking at her watch since she didn't want to be late for the bus that would take her to her second job. It was clear that she loved both of her sons — there should be a way to acknowledge and reward parents like that — yet there were few choices she could afford even though she was trying her best. Feeling guilty I tried to explain to her that we had only a limited number of slots and that because Joseph had been involved with the police he had gotten priority.

"But I don't want Landon to get involved with the police! I need this other job and I can't watch him after school. I'm afraid if he doesn't get into your program, he *will* get in trouble!"

Memories of Richard and Ben flooded my mind. Landon was eligible for my program, but future funding was dictated by showing we served the "most in need." Landon simply didn't look as needy as others. I tried to think about other programs that Landon could join, but all the youth programs worked the same way. We all compete to bring in the "neediest," so enrolling as yet untroubled kids like Landon or Ben, even if they might otherwise be eligible, was a liability in terms of getting future funding to continue the program.

She pressed me. "Joseph got in trouble again and was sent to a program where he got a tutor and was offered a scholarship if he applied for college. So now Landon thinks that the only way he can get to college is to get in trouble like his brother." Her words made me sick to my stomach but I still didn't enroll Landon. I needed my funding! But I knew that this scenario was repeated throughout the social services sector every day. I began to wonder if maybe the problem in the social sector wasn't with the programs but with those that funded them. Still as the director of a nonprofit I found it almost impossible to not bend to the interests of my funders. *I began to resent our funders.*

The Josephs' of the world need second or even third chances, make no mistake about that. But with so few incentives for kids that do the right thing, we are making *social programs a race to the bottom.* My thoughts began to move towards the development of the missing system that would invest directly in Ben's talents or Landon's desire to go to college. Why did Landon first have to get in trouble to get a scholarship?

The rules for nonprofits were the inverse of what seemed common sense to me. Clara Miller, President of the Heron Foundation, seemed to have experienced this contradiction when running the Nonprofit Finance Fund and lending to non-profits. She wrote in her 2005 Nonprofit Quarterly article entitled, *The Looking Glass World of Nonprofit Money*; "But enter the nonprofit sector, and it's a new and irrational world, like stepping through a looking glass. The [business] rules, when they apply at all, are reversed, and the science turns topsy-turvy."

Nonprofits must please their funders ahead of pleasing their clients.

Customers are "recipients" that have to show their worst side rather than their talents.

Philanthropy and Government could reduce the need for welfare or charity by creating a system of support based on strengths. The *alternative* has to target the funders to change their practices since the nonprofits will follow those who control their funding.

It was hard to reconcile the contradiction of how I ran my personal life and how differently I was expected to run social service programs. But again, funders played a role. To get funding I had to convince the donors or foundations that my staff — my programs — are what led to the change in our clients' lives. We implied or even claimed that without us, without the services we imposed, the parents or guardians could not make progress or the make the right decisions.

Sadly, even the families participating in these programs start to question their own competence as they promote themselves as needy.

Linda from her experiences with welfare and nonprofit service programs:

> … if you consult programs often then you begin to believe their way is the only way, because you are told so much that you are not valuable…. It discourages people, even though they have a lot of talent and ideas.

Sandy was seeking assistance for one of their nine children:

> They just kept telling us we had to wait and wait. So then my husband got injured and that was the only way we got into the system. You have to be sick to get assistance? I don't understand.

Linda on how she felt families like hers should be involved:

> It doesn't consist of just having a focus group, then they go and dis-

cuss you on their own. We have to allow people to be really active in their own destiny.

We are stuck in a vicious cycle. Foundations and donors want to help those in need so the nonprofits and government agencies provide data depicting the families as needy. That in turn reinforces the funder's impression that the families cannot change without institutional help, so they continue to fund based on the extent of neediness, thus forcing agencies to generate data on more problems with the community and so on. It really has become a self-perpetuating *race to the bottom*. And it just fuels the stereotype that people like Linda, Sandy, my mother, and my sister are not capable of managing their lives without programs.

CHAPTER SIX

Us and Them

"The walls are just high enough so the people we are talking about can't hear us talking about them"

At a conference in New York held by the group, Opportunity Nation, I was asked to be on a panel about closing the "opportunity gap". In these settings, everyone speaks of the folks that cycle in and out of poverty as the "disadvantaged", the "poor", the "underserved" or more generically, "them". Sadly, as a panelist, I found myself also differentiating "us" from "them" in one of the workshops.

But then an older man in the audience interrupted us and introduced himself as a pastor of a church near New Orleans. He never gave his name but with the measured tones of a preacher he lectured us that we have to stop using labels like "disadvantaged". "The very fact of labeling creates problems" he said about how we separate ourselves from one another. "They are just human beings like the rest of us". *He was so right.*

Another panelist, Kirsten Lodal added, "as soon as we start talking about low-income families we use a whole different vocabulary that we never, ever, would apply to people in the upper income classes."

She continued, "I'm not self-sufficient, nor is anyone here. I can't tell you how much it takes to keep my own life together — but I get praised and rewarded when I seek help." I wish I had said that!

The problem created by designating a large segment of our society as "different" is two-fold. First, it implies that those folks respond to life situations differently than "us", those with privilege, and so we put aside the common-sense expectations we use every day in our own lives. Since we then think that we don't understand "them", we test new theories of change and unrealistic practices, doing to "them" what would not be acceptable to "us". The way my social service programs were structured was not attractive to my family make no sense to middle and upper income families. I came to realize that I wouldn't put my nephew and nieces through my own programs, even as they faced the same situations as those I did admit to my programs. As a middle-class person, if I pay for a service, that service provider needs to please me as the consumer. It doesn't work that way for nonprofit or government programs. Therefore, if the programs we explore at these conferences aren't good enough for our own families, why put others through them?

The second reason why we wouldn't want that vocabulary applied to "us" is that the words have negative connotations. Being labeled "poor" implies that you are flawed, likely not working hard enough. Disadvantaged is also a paternalistic term that implies the need for advantaged outsiders to show you how to overcome the disadvantages. All of the terms as they are currently used imply the need for outsiders to tell a low-income family what to do. These terms separate us from one another.

After the reverend, Kirsten, and I challenged the terminology I hoped that this spark of controversy would change the tenor of the conversation. But on the very next question the panel and audience were back to the 'us' and 'them' paradigm. Attitudes are often so deep-seated that even when people agree they fall right back into the accepted nomenclature and thinking.

It is frustrating how our society and those that want to be helpful keep depicting people that have less almost like lab rats to be experimented on. At that workshop we spoke of how needy "they" were and our new theories or innovative programs to help "them". Some discussed how they would test the effectiveness of an intervention by providing services to one group while denying the services to another group, the control group. Doing control group evaluations, as if my family and neighbors were lab rats, was the greatest insult. Did I have some disease when I was growing up poor, and did I suddenly get well when I became middle class? *You don't solve poverty by treating it as some mysterious disease and we just need to find the right vaccine.*

Before quitting AND and my social service programs in 2001, I had a staff of over 100 social workers, employment specialists and fundraisers. That number of staff forced us to develop an internal email system so that staff could confer across sites. Over time I noticed that I would see emails such as "I have a friend moving here from Cambridge. Does anyone know of any housing or part time job opportunities?" Most of us use our social networks for advice and referrals, and most jobs and the best housing opportunities are found through social networks. As pointed out previously, only a small percentage of the best opportunities show up in the newspaper or online.

One day I assembled my counseling staff and asked why, since they were charged to help our program clients to find jobs or housing, I never saw them use the staff network to find jobs or housing for them. Everyone looked a bit puzzled that I would ask that but I asked them to try to tap our staff networks for our clients. For a few weeks, I monitored the emails but saw only a few outreach emails asking for help through our staff networks and then it all died out. A month or so later I got everyone together again and asked what happened. This time I did get a reply.

"It is hard to keep a professional distance from our clients if we involve them in our personal networks" was the reply. In discussion, everyone agreed that the social networks of my over one hundred staff provided the best opportunities but professionalism required keeping a distance from our clients. It was clear that professionalization of interactions perpetuates the social class divide.

Respect is where it starts

Respect is of paramount importance and treating "others" as different from "us", the more privileged, is disrespectful. In olden time duals were fought if you were disrespected. Very often kids join gangs as a way to force respect. Racism, sexism, classism, homophobia, all embody disrespect. Respect can't be solved by passing policies or legislation. If a policy is passed by 51 percent, it still means that 49 percent disagree. When that one kid called me a "chink" in the sixth grade it wouldn't have made me feel better to know that 49 percent of my classmates felt like he did. In the 1960s, the Civil Rights Act didn't increase respect or solve racism. It did not make it a level playing field or reduce the privilege of the well off. For those facing racism, it is a huge barrier. Others see progress and assume racism is not a significant problem. A poll done by CNN in 2015, fifty years after the passage of the Civil Rights Act, found that only 49 percent of the population thought racism was a big problem; half of those in our country feel that the racially charged comments in the 2016 presidential campaign were acceptable enough to elect Donald Trump. A significant portion of our country apparently wonders why racially based protests continue.

Political correctness too often hides the depth of the divide in this country. Our society has to address that divide with more than policies. We have to tell the true story of how our lowest income residents contribute to society, overcoming barriers. We have to celebrate their sacrifices and resourcefulness, not their weaknesses.

For my mother, then my sister, and me, pride and respect are huge. That is what keeps us going, keeps us determined. That is typical for anyone, rich or poor. We all want to raise our teenagers to have pride and self-confidence. We surround our children with those that are respectful of them and will reinforce their positive sides, as well as our authority as parents. Imagine raising children under tough economic circumstances and on top of that be hearing a constant stream of negative messages about you as a parent or negative comments about your community, culture or religion. Raising strong, confident, young people just becomes that much harder when your culture or you as a parent or guardian are denigrated.

Our leaders and experts

Newt Gingrich, a presidential candidate in 2010, talked about how the "very poor don't know how to get up and work for 8 hours. They've never seen anyone around them work…" He never lived in my neighborhoods and must not have read the census studies cited earlier. Another presidential candidate depicted those with lower income as "dependent" on government. The comments made by Donald Trump characterizing Mexican immigrants living here as likely criminals and rapists would have both hurt and infuriated my mother.

But those on the more liberal-leaning part of the political spectrum also depict low-income families as flawed. They will argue that we need programs to help them be good parents.

At a Washington Post video event on March 7, 2013, I sat on a panel discussing poverty issues[17]. There I heard Jared Bernstein, a Brookings Institute Fellow and formerly the policy advisor to Vice President Biden, justifying the role of government programs by claiming that "good decisions are essential…[but] a lot of people *don't have the right parents*" to make those decisions. He continued, and "even if they have good parents," — hopefully he would have included my mother — "they are facing a different economic structure," implying that 'they' are not smart enough to figure their way through our changing economic order. The rest of the panelists nodded their approval and it appeared that all of the panel, except me, would likely trust a twenty-two-year old Harvard graduate with no life experience to make better decisions about poverty issues than a parent who had navigated our toughest neighborhoods with very little income. No one was willing to acknowledge the heroic resourcefulness it takes to overcome the limited choices faced by the parents they were disparaging. *Those of privilege primarily trust others with privilege.*

---

17 The Washington Post Live series in 2013. See the Notes section for a link to the video.

Jared appeared to be the most liberal on the panel that included Ron Haskins who became the policy advisor to Republican majority leader Paul Ryan and represented the more conservative voice. Ron and Jared seemed to agree on the perspective that lower income families are less capable than "us".

This unity of *experts* bolsters arguments by others even more radical, such as conservative commentator Bill O'Reilly who wrote in May 2015 that "we should have a war against chaotic, irresponsible parents — addictive behavior, laziness, apathy…" ending with "I clearly blame irresponsible parents for much of the poverty in the U.S.A. and the situation is getting worse." All of these *experts* missed the census data cited in chapter two showing that only about 3 percent stay in poverty more than three or four years and many of those are elderly or have permanent disabilities. They missed seeing the work of the janitor cleaning up after us or the security guard at the door.

So how do you raise a child in a society where the leading voices across the political spectrum put you down as a parent?

Always behind their back

In my over 35 years of working in the nonprofit social service sector I have attended dozens of conferences to discuss issues of poverty. One held annually in Mexico, Opportunity Collaboration, takes place at a Club Med by the beach. A number of us that have attended find it troubling that we all continue to go to this luxurious place to discuss "them", those in poverty. One of the workshop leaders said that once in describing where he was going to a friend, said:

"I'm going to a conference about poverty being held at a Club Med in Mexico where the walls are just high enough so that the people we are talking about can't hear us talking about them." That was the perfect description.

It is amazing how many conferences are held to talk about those in poverty and the very people we are talking about are excluded — or are only there as examples of success for a social service program. FII is often asked to bring one or two families to show our effectiveness and we generally ask "can we bring 20 families to be speakers or to run a workshop so that the usual suspects, "us", can hear their perspective?"

Our requests have been turned down until a conference in 2015 held by Citizens University in Seattle. The conference organizer, Eric Liu, said "sure, bring thirty!" and so we did. They lowered the entrance fee to $25 for the families and we put out a notice to all the FII families to see who wanted to attend. They would have to pay the $25 fee but within limits we would cover flight and hotel for two nights. To our surprise, we got over seventy applications to go even though some would have to miss work. We chose thirty from six different cities and the families held a workshop to share their perspective with other attendees which included policy makers, funders, and service program professionals. It was a great success that we hope will be replicated at other conferences so that families can speak for themselves.

One of the things I learned from U.C. Berkeley watching 3,000 students surrounding a police car is that there is strength in numbers. If we had just one or two families in these conferences they would have felt isolated, powerless. But if there are five, ten, fifty peer families, their power grows and collectively they can change the conversation about how their lives should be seen. They can be equals in the conversation. *Collectively they are no longer the excluded, disempowered, "them".*

The "Us and Them" in behavioral studies

Scientists have been studying behavior for decades. The studies applied to "us", those with a privileged social status, highlight what author Daniel Pink points out in his lectures and his book, *Drive,* that there is a *"deep human need to direct our own lives, to learn and create new things, and to do better by ourselves and our world."* Referring to decades of scientific research on human motivation, studies have consistently identified that self-direction leads to better performance than carrots or stick rewards. Offering food, training, or even money as incentives doesn't improve performance, but *actually slows* it. Having enough choices to direct your own life is what works. Pink continues summarizing years of studies that *"The urge to direct our own lives",* not rewards, leads to the best outcomes. Those of us in privileged positions believe this and feel entitled to direct our own lives. We want jobs and opportunities to create. This is such an American value, but we don't apply it to "them".

The behavioral studies about the poor being cited in books such as *Scarcity* and research studies, such as *Poverty Interrupted*[18] published by Ideas42, ignore the studies on motivation and effectiveness to which Daniel Pink refers. It's as if the studies around giving people choices and control over decisions only apply to "us" and not to "them".

Poverty Interrupted got a lot of attention in the nonprofit sector because it bolstered the case for the role of providing top-down solutions.

---

18   See the Notes section for links to these publications.

The study tries to connect the scarcity and stress faced by low-income families to an inability to see options; they called it "tunnel vision." That paper also asserts the widely-held stereotype that scarcity leads to bad decisions and a loss of self-control. Like Jared, Ron, and the other panelist at the *Washington Post* event, this study promotes the idea that social programs are needed to direct or lead the decisions families have to make. All of these *experts* propose that top-down intervention, programs and policies, is a way of reducing stress since it frees families from having to make as many decisions. Proposing the primacy of top-down solutions just deepens the societal belief that the families I grew up with, or now work with, are not smart enough or good enough to figure out their own lives.

In *Poverty Interrupted* they write that "scarcity makes [them] less insightful, less forward-thinking, and less controlled". *Less controlled, really?* These conclusions are from what are likely liberal researchers. They then take that perspective and propose that "the burden of change rests primarily with the individuals and organizations who have the power to design programs and systems…". These behaviorists get attention from nonprofits and their funders because they provide another basis to continue top-down control and exclude families from leading their own change. They bolster the assertion by the Black Panthers about poverty pimping. It is a self-serving perspective by those already in power.

Taking control away from people, or trying to induce them with carrots or sticks, is the opposite of the conclusions from the decades of studies that Daniel Pink referenced. It is the opposite of what most of us with privilege would accept. However well-meaning, those promoting more direction from those in power are feeding into the same stereotypes promoted by those that are bigots. Their paternalism gives those like Bill O'Reilly or Donald Trump the underpinnings to support their assertions that poor judgement by low-income families is what has led to their situation.

Then what is the reality? If you had measured my sister's stress and ability to make decisions right after she got beat up and maybe for a few days after, it is true that she was not forward thinking, maybe had tunnel vision and she needed advice and the support of a social service worker. But, as with my mother, after a few days she gathered herself and began to plan and make logical decisions for the future. Raquel and my mother didn't lose their smarts because of a crisis and they were not the exceptions.

My mother was under chronic stress, yet she got me into and thru U.C. Berkeley. With three children and little financial support from our family, my sister had very few good options but made the best decisions she could under the circumstances. *She didn't have permanent tunnel vision, she just didn't have options.* She certainly didn't want a program to take away more control of her life. Taking decisions and options away from my sister is how Chuck kept power over her. It is how slave owners controlled their slaves. That is how society can keep power in the hands of a few, even if some are well intentioned.

The Whitehall Studies:

In the 1990s I became aware of behavioral studies that backed my personal experiences that having choices to control my life is what actually relieved my stress. The Whitehall studies[19] were started in 1985 by Mi-

---

19   See the Notes section for links to further information about these studies.

chael Marmot at University College London to investigate the importance of social class on people's health. His Stress & Health Study followed more than 10,000 working men and women and the studies continue to this day.

Marmot's study compared people in high-level management positions with those in lower-level positions, even janitors. They measured the levels of cortisol which is released when someone is stressed. The more stress someone experiences the more cortisol is released. What the researchers found was surprising and they spent years trying to explain it. They found that the lower-level staff, the janitors and clerks, released more cortisol than the high-level managers who worked long hours and had tremendous responsibilities. They finally concluded that the determining factor was the level of control each felt over their work environment. The janitors doing routine work clearly were more stressed than top managers with heavy responsibilities but more choices. Other studies added to the picture, finding the lack of options at home or other situations also added to stress. Yes, scarcity creates stress but the solution is not structure or programs taking over decisions or even rewards decided on by outsiders. The janitor's jobs were fully structured to reduce decisions by the janitors and yet the janitors were stressed even if their home was stable. Stress reduction requires fulfillment; having access to the choices that enable us to take control of our lives. The well-off are given choices because they have money and with their social networks they are often able to shape their jobs and lives. It is not the amount of work or number of decisions, but the control and fulfillment you have in life that reduces stress.

Many join the nonprofit sector at low wages because they get to be creative and solve things for others. It is fulfilling work and being fulfilled is joyful, thus it reduces stress. But the helpers seldom realize that they diminish the fulfillment, thus disempower, the very people they want to help. The interference by those in more powerful social positions can actually diminish progress, as Daniel Pink pointed out. The *alternative* has to get helpers to step back and trust the families with choices so they can take control over their lives.

CHAPTER SEVEN

Undermining Family and Village
'Paternalists advance people's interests
at the expense of their liberty'

The *alternative* being proposed lies between, or outside of, the perspectives of those from the political right and left. So many of the fights across the political spectrum seem artificial. One side claims "family" and the other side "village". Or the demarcation line may be between personal responsibility versus government responsibility. The fact is that all of these "issues" of demarcation are interrelated so fighting over who is right is useless. As a child of poverty who went on to work in poor communities, I have learned that there is a role for everyone in the building of strong communities, building a strong healthy society, including government and the private sector, even if we don't like their current role. Family or close caring relationships lay the foundation for a person's success, but to grow and participate in the wider world you need a village. We all, rich or poor, want to control our own lives and are willing to take personal responsibility as long as we set the table. Sadly, those on the political right and left agree on one thing: neither trusts low-income parents or guardians to lead their own change. While there are criticisms across the political spectrum, this chapter focuses primarily on the failings of those, who like me, are working on issues of poverty and equity.

*

Undermining parental authority - 1983

We had just finished a great counseling session with Myong Nguyen when she chased after my colleague and me as we departed her building. "Don't help me anymore!" she said in agitated, broken English. "My children are not respecting me!"

Myong had always been so agreeable when we counseled her. I didn't understand why she was upset. She didn't understand the school system or the options for her teenage son who was starting to get in trouble. I thought our advice had been helpful.

It was 1983 and I was two years into my job as executive director of AND in San Francisco. The social worker and I had gone to Myong's apartment because AND had received government funding to provide counseling to refugees from the Vietnam War. Many settled in crowded residential hotels or small apartments in San Francisco's Chinatown and Tenderloin neighborhoods. Life was hard for the refugees as they tried to transition into a new culture and a new home.

That afternoon, I was training a new 26-year-old counselor with a master's degree in social work from U.C. Berkeley. We went to Myong's three-room apartment in the Tenderloin, one of San Francisco's roughest neighborhoods. I watched as my young social worker counseled Myong who was probably in her forties. I sat on a couch stacked with sheets and blankets, most likely a bed for one of Myong's three children. The social worker sat at the table with Myong.

Out of the dark of an adjoining room, Myong's 15-year-old son, Tae, appeared and leaned against the door. Tae was being actively recruited by one of the Chinatown gangs and my colleagues and I were afraid for him and his two younger siblings. As he heard the conversation his face took on a look of disgust. My social worker was asking Myong to set goals, timelines, and identify markers of success. I assumed that Tae's disgust was aimed at my staffer. I didn't realize his scowl was directed at his mother, and that we had done harm to her stature as a parent and their relationship.

It is difficult to tell a well-intentioned professional that they may actually be doing their client more harm than good but Myong made that harm clear in her words and body language that afternoon. Her rage didn't fully make sense until we found out a week later that Tae had run away and was staying with members of the Wah Ching gang in Chinatown. While there were probably many factors affecting her son's decision, I worried that our insistence on meeting at her place and my social worker's intervention was the last straw in the frayed relationship between Myong and Tae. Tae had been attending some of the youth activities we ran and my staff had heard him complain about his mother. Just as many people thought my mother was a bad parent because of what happened to Raquel, my staff and I privately blamed Myong for the trouble her son was getting into. And just as my mother sobbed when she lost my sister to an abusive man, I'm sure Myong was just as devastated to lose Tae to a gang.

When Myong would not return our calls we started to ask friends how she was. It was from Myong's friends that we learned her full story; how, at the end of the Vietnam War she had led her children across the Mekong River in the middle of the night. Two people with them died in the crossing. Myong had already lost her husband, a soldier for the South Vietnamese army, during the war. Still she managed to flee to a refugee camp in Thailand and braved pirates at sea to get her children to the United States. Her journey and arrival in America took an immense amount of intelligence and resourcefulness. At that point, her children admired her just as I admired my mother's determination.

But once she arrived her stature as an authority figure and a parent began to diminish. When they first arrived in the U.S. Myong applied for welfare and other refugee support services. It seemed like a logical choice but prevailing negative stereotypes diminished her social status, especially to her children — and what were supposed to be helpful programs contributed to that diminishment. My mother avoided welfare and charity partly because she felt it would diminish her in my eyes and with others.

We learned that right after we left Myong's apartment that day, Tae had called her "stupid", a dynamic that had been going on for a while. She understood how his watching her taking direction from outsiders only confirmed his view of her. She resented that every counselor — she had three counselors, each from different agencies — gave her advice and asked her to set goals which sometimes were in conflict with one another. They then monitored her as if she wasn't disciplined enough to do the right thing. Unwilling to be anything but polite, she tried to comply and be grateful.

Myong shared with her friends that while she needed some of the information our counselors provided, her children were beginning to believe the messages they heard from the larger society that she wasn't capable of making good decisions. Moreover, the ongoing put-downs her children heard at school and on TV about refugees and people of color were making them feel ashamed of her, themselves, and their culture.

She turned away from our program and all social service programs. Instead, she forged friendships with other families like hers, seeking help from other refugees who had successfully navigated the systems to which she needed access. Spending time with those families not only helped her gain knowledge and examples of how to make things work for her in this country, but it also provided emotional support. This new community of friends created a sort of village for her younger children, the kind she had left behind in Vietnam. With this new village she hoped to win Tae back.

Myong's story was one of my first lessons about the primary role of peers and is one of the most fundamental building blocks of the *alternative*.

I learned one other difficult lesson from Tae's story. He had quickly realized that our youth workers had access to more of the things he wanted than his mother did. Our program took him to his first baseball game and on trips outside of San Francisco. His mother didn't even have a car. We could provide school supplies and games. My counselors lent a sympathetic ear if he complained about his mom. Just as my mother couldn't provide Raquel with the dresses she wanted in order to fit in with her school friends, so Tae's mother couldn't offer the new American life he wanted. As a rebellious teenager, Tae paid more respect to my staff than to the woman who braved pirates and gunfire to get him here.

Should youth programs stop taking at-risk kids on field trips? Probably not in all cases, but I have come to realize that if we gave parents the money we spend providing all of these amenities to their kids, they could afford to take their own youngsters to ballgames and trips. The *alternative* being demonstrated by FII provides matching funds for efforts by the parents so that they can be the primary providers for their kids and have a chance to strengthen their relationships. The data collected by FII shows that providing dollars that match the efforts of families to spend time together is one of the most sought after resource accessed by enrolled families. Also, just as FII strives to empower and involve the adults in a household, there are new program approaches that are beginning to do the same. A foster care program in Hawaii, *Ohana*, makes parents and relatives central to their services. Programs using a *"restorative justice"* approach include family and friends to reduce criminal recidivism. *Working with and empowering families, parents, extended family or guardians is the future of social work.*

A friend, Kouichoy Saechao, is part of the Iu Mien refugees that came from Laos after the war in Vietnam. He recounted how his community in America had similar experiences to that of Myong and her Vietnamese neighbors. The Mien had strong clan ties in their home country but those strong ties and family structures began to break down here in the United States. For a period in the 1990s, Kouichoy shared that Iu Mien youth had the highest incarceration rate of any ethnic group in Oakland, California. Describing why so many of the Mien teenagers had gravitated to gangs, he told the story of a mother's visit with her teen to his probation officer. As the meeting started she told her son to pull up his pants and sit up straight. The probation officer intervened. "No, it's ok here in America," he told her in front of her son, dismissing her parental authority with a wave of his hand. Later, when she tried to discipline her son or keep him home at night, he would just respond that it was done differently in America. Kouichoy told me this happened all the time when the parents tried to 'parent' in front of social workers, teachers or other professionals. Parental authority in the family began to break down and programs like mine added to that breakdown. I don't believe most wealthy parents would ever allow a program staffer to dismiss their orders to their children; why do we do that to others, to "them"?

"In our country, we lost our country. In this country, we lost our soul", was how Kouichoy described his community's experience in the United States.

*

Implicit bias thru subtle messages

In the first presidential candidate debate in 2016 between Donald Trump and Hillary Clinton, Hillary was asked about racism within the nation's police forces. She responded: "I think *implicit bias* is a problem for everyone, not just the police." Implicit bias refers to unconscious attitudes or stereotypes that affect our actions and decisions. We are often unaware of actions we take that add to the negative stereotype of low-income parents and guardians. You don't have to be an overt racist to add to the prejudice families already face. The following example was so subtle that it took me quite a while to understand why I was upset.

She got an A-minus! She got an A-minus! I can't believe it! It's so great! I'm so proud of her! So happy! I can't believe it!" Joan, the young director of a women's mentorship program, went on like that all evening at a dinner meeting of Eureka Fellowship recipients. Joan received the news about the grade on her cell phone as I arrived and she was so beside herself with joy that she barely said hello. "An A-minus!" was her amazed refrain. Joan couldn't concentrate on the food because she was so happy for Josephina, a forty-something year-old single mother of three, and a client in her agency's women's group for low-income mothers.

While the executive directors of other social service agencies were congratulating her, I was getting a bit ill. It took a little intro-spection to arrive at why I became so offended by the big deal Joan was making of Josephina's good grade, and then it hit me. Josephina was a Latina, just like my mother. Emphasizing the A-minus gave everyone the impression that Josephina must not be very smart at all or this wouldn't be such a big deal. That's what people presumed about my mother because she only had a third-grade education in Mexico. My mother was as smart as anyone and always thought of herself as capable of more than an A-minus. What if Josephina had the capacity to get an A+ but Joan never recognized it? In that case if Joan acted this excited in front of Josephina about an A- it would have been a put-down. Wouldn't it have been better to assume that Josephina was a smart, capable, solid A student, who almost got there? That would be a well-placed compliment.

This incident appears minor, just as the probation officer's action or excluding low-income families from poverty conferences seem minor. Those who come from more privileged backgrounds don't recognize the continuous, often small, negative messages sent to those of lower social status. Those negative messages accumulate and eat at one's identity because it isn't just the well-intentioned who feed negative messages to the Josephinas of our world. Those in power will portray parents as neglectful, the "wrong parents" or even as likely "criminals and rapists"! It is sad when those who want to be helpful, who feel empathy, reflect similar negative assumptions through misguided sympathy or compliments.

Racism, gender bias, classism, homophobia, undocumented status, and all of the other stereotypical prejudices that are ingrained in our society often come out innocently. We must confront our internalized prejudices openly if we are to resolve them. In a conference plenary speech Alicia Garza, a leading activist in the "Black Lives Matter" movement, pointed out that we can't just focus on policy. "There has to be a cultural shift" if we want the laws and policies to mean something. Well-intended social sector colleagues need to recognize the assumptions they have internalized if they seek to confront all the 'isms. To overcome our prejudice, we have to actively look for the strengths and talents of those we wish to help.

In a conversation with Suzan-Lori Parks, winner of the Pulitzer Prize and the MacArthur "genius" award, I was explaining the progress that groups of Asian, Black and Hispanic families had made in Oakland. When I told her that over a two-year period the income of the black families had jumped over 37 percent and the income of the Asians had only jumped 18 percent, a look of surprise passed over her face. She had clearly prepared herself to hear the opposite. I asked her why she was surprised that the black families did so well. She went on to explain that she, and many of her community, had internalized society's message of low expectations for her community. "We've internalized the racism we have faced," she said.

As Penn State Black Caucus President Holman put it "One little comment barely makes an impact, but repeated offenses over time can wear at the victim and tear them down". I'm sure Joan and the other directors at that dinner would assume it was just one little comment because they likely didn't live under the cloud and stream of such comments, small and large. It is not about intent, or being a nice person. Joan is a very nice person, and so are the researchers who wrote "Poverty Interrupted".

If we want the world to be a better, more inclusive place, we need to approach each other across class, race, and other divides with a positive mindset. *You can't be helpful to someone if you are unconsciously influenced by your perception of their weaknesses.* If we look closely at those on the bottom of our economic ladder, at "them", we will discover that the vast majority of people are amazingly resourceful and contribute tremendously to society. They are not takers — if anything, they are a population exploited by those at the top.

Genocide by Stereotype

If American society held a non-paternalistic, or better, a positive, unbiased view of the working poor, then Joan's "compliment" to her client would not risk a negative reaction. But if you are from a lower socio-economic class, you not only struggle to live on poverty wages, but also must fight to keep your pride intact when so many, even the kindest, assume you are less than capable. Writing about paternalism, philosophy professor Peter Suber, now with the Harvard Open Access Project, argues, "Paternalism is a temptation in every arena of life where people hold power over others." He continues: "Paternalists advance people's interests (such as life, health, or safety) at the expense of their liberty. In this, paternalists suppose that they can make wiser decisions than the people for whom they act. Sometimes this is based on presumptions about their own wisdom or the foolishness of other people, and can be dismissed as presumptuous. But sometimes it is not."

I quote Suber here because I believe presumptions by my professional colleagues in the social service sector have hindered the War on poverty. The fact is that many of us have control over — but do not fully understand — the social and economic experiences that make up the world of those we try to help. Thus, we are constantly in danger of doing more harm than good. The acknowledgment Joan had hoped to offer her client may not have been a bad act in itself, but Josephina had probably spent a lifetime absorbing negative messages and we should not take a chance that we might continue to diminish her self-confidence or stature further.

Some professionals have recognized this dangerous strain of paternalism in the social service sector and have fought to change the traditional language of "handouts" to the idea of offering families a "hand up." My view is that this change in terminology isn't much of an improvement; it still promotes the idea that the outside helper is the key and knows better. Another popular saying in the social service sector is "give a man a fish and you feed him for a day; teach a man to fish and you feed him for a lifetime." Again, the starting assumption is that the man is not capable and therefore needs to be taught. Most don't consider the real possibility that the man might already know how to fish, or can learn on his own, but only needs money for the equipment, or space, or time to make the choice for himself — or in my mother's case, for herself.

What is a non-partisan constant is the exclusion of any option that would involve a person's own agency; they might have their own ideas of how to live and would rather just have access to a little of what we spend trying to help them so they could pick their own destination.

SECTION II

The Alternative

Put families in the driver's seat

CHAPTER EIGHT

Following Peer Paths
"That's not the way it's done!"

Many of us don't know what to do to get ahead, whether we are rich or poor. Our futures and actions are heavily influenced by those around us. The natural human tendency is to observe others and follow those whose successful actions interest us. Paths or solutions are not acts of individuality but are heavily dependent on others, especially if those that are successful are willing to share their experiences and it becomes a common goal or collective action. I began to learn about mutuality by watching families who were *not* enrolled in my social service programs.

*

Paths already forged

"I have to quit now. It's my turn to go to college" my bookkeeper, May, declared with a hint of regret in leaving us. May Cheung had worked with me at AND for almost a decade. She started as a clerk like my mother and eventually became one of our bookkeepers. Also, like my mother, May had always been ambitious, but her life had been put on hold while her newly immigrated family from Hong Kong rebuilt their lives in a new country. I knew that her role in the family was similar to mine. She and I had both been designated as the helpers for siblings in the family.

Over the decade that May worked with me, her father worked as a dishwasher in one of San Francisco's Chinatown restaurants while her mother sewed in one of Chinatown's basement garment sweatshops. These were ugly, dead-end jobs where they were being exploited. Her father worked extremely long hours starting mid-morning and not finishing till things were cleaned up well after dinner, and I would be surprised if he earned minimum wage. The sweat shops where her mother worked were notorious for bad working conditions, and since workers were paid by the piece sewn, it was difficult to earn a decent wage. This family was like so many of the other poor immigrant families that my agency was trying to help.

One of our ideas seemed obvious: if her mother or father were willing to learn a minimal amount of vocational English we could get them better jobs that required just a little English. Twice my agency started "Vocational English" classes for Chinese speakers, but had a hard time filling the classes. We finally talked May's father into joining the class, but like almost all the others he stopped coming and I was curious as to why.

With May translating, I asked why he and others dropped the class. He looked embarrassed and hesitant to be critical.

"It's not the way it is done!" he finally blurted out in Cantonese. I was totally puzzled.

"What is not done that way?" I asked.

"We want our children to go to college like the other families," was his answer.

I still didn't understand, and he wasn't able to explain further, but I began to see that he was following a path set by others before him. A number of years before she left our employ May had told me that her family and two other families were moving from the residential hotels in Chinatown to the Inner Richmond district in San Francisco to share a single flat. It was a step others had taken. I had seen this sharing before, where a newly arrived family first rents a couple rooms in a Chinatown tenement, gets to know other families and then they share the rental of a flat. Shortly before May quit she told me they were taking the next step in the pattern. Together with another family they were pooling their savings and income to buy a house in San Francisco's Sunset district and renovate the garage into a rental unit for income. She and I already knew that the next step would be for the families to use the equity from that first house to purchase a separate house or help their kids purchase a home on their own.

Her siblings were also following a path, now finishing college just as the kids were of the other families they had befriended. May's family sur-rounded itself with others who shared a similar vision, helped one another and set the expectations for all the kids. Success for them was a collective effort of a path laid out by families before them.

Just as my mother's choices had confused me, I didn't initially un-derstand why May's parents accepted exploitative jobs or took little in-terest in assimilating into an English-speaking society. As with Myong, I initially felt her parents were making the wrong decisions, just as Jared Bernstein and Ron Haskins might have assumed. My colleagues and I kept coming up with new programs and new theories of change, never understanding her family and their cultural decisions. But cultures and subcultures often develop their own paths to success and the reasons may never be clear to outsiders. I couldn't understand, but I also couldn't argue with their success.

Though it had taken a decade before May could go to college, it was clear they would all succeed. We were offering them what we thought would be obvious training and program help, but it might have been better if instead we had diverted the funds we used for training and just matched the savings that her parents had focused on. They were already taking initiative for their future and thus had "skin in the game". The *alternative* is set up to discover, then match people's efforts, especially when they already have committed significant time or dollars.

Forging a new path for their youth

In the mid-1990s, gang wars erupted between two groups of Iu Mien youth from Oakland and those from Richmond, California. As described earlier, the Iu Mien families, much like the better known Hmong people, are refugees from the war in Vietnam. They had monitored the Ho Chi Minh trail for the CIA during the war and most fled Laos after the American's pulled out of Vietnam. Just like Myong and her family, many made their way to refugee camps in Thailand and finally arrived in the U.S. In Laos, their survival depended on slash-and-burn farming as well as payments from the CIA. But in the United States, with no written language or marketable skills, the large majority of newcomers turned to welfare and refugee programs.

Those that successfully made the arduous trek to the United States were considered resourceful, even heroic — but as the years passed they found that they were looked down upon because of their refugee status and limited knowledge of American culture. Their youth would hide that they were Mien and began to distance themselves from their families by joining gangs. During that period when you read of a shooting around Oakland, it most often involved Iu Mien youth. In the U.S., the fabric of the Mien as a close community was falling apart, and gangs were becoming their children's new "community." Joining a gang became the expectation of every young Mien male as they grew up.

During that period, I was running the AND youth gang programs that Richard had joined. Our program was trying to curb the violence. The Oakland police had set up a gang task force. Yet it was clear that outsider interventions were not stopping the shootings.

Then on the evening of July 18, 1997, my friend, Kouichoy Saechao, got a call telling him that his seven-year-old nephew, Sou Sio, had been killed in a drive-by shooting a few miles from his house. Devastated, Kouichoy, along with other local parents, knew that the gang problem was not being solved by the police or by programs like mine. They began to talk among themselves realizing that their youth had lost respect for their parents and culture. None of the youth wanted to be known as part of the Iu Mien community and their language and cultural traditions were rapidly disappearing.

Kouichoy and the other elders facilitated several meetings amongst the parents and other relatives of the gang-involved youth. As the anger subsided the families and youth discovered their commonalities. Some of the rivals were cousins. But the authority of the parents had eroded. It was not helpful for the parents to meet alone with their own kids at times.

So instead, groups of parents met with the kids to explain how much they all cared for them. The gatherings were not to yell or punish the young men but to demonstrate the concern and love everyone, not just their parents, felt for them — something that their American schools and programs couldn't offer. It was akin to the love that my former client, Richard, discovered when he met his future wife, Marina, as well as her circle of friends.

Michelle Chao, who is Iu Mien and came to work with me when FII was formed, recounted how the parents took control to save their own youth. The parents decided that they, as a community, needed to rebuild pride in their culture and give their young people an alternative to the gangs. They wanted their kids to consider college so they started a scholarship fund by collecting donations of $25 to $50 dollars from other families. They then had a community-wide celebration where a few scholarships of $500 were presented to local students. Given the costs of college even then, it was not a lot of money, but the award ceremonies were symbols of the community's support for their children. The fact so many very poor neighbors and families contributed meant much more than the money.

Instilling pride in the Iu Mien culture was another significant task. Though most parents were on welfare, they still saved what they could and pooled their resources to buy a piece of land in East Oakland with a dilapidated house that became a community center. To this day, contributions from Iu Mien families pays the monthly mortgage. The city has also built centers in East Oakland that have youth programs and the Mayor along with philanthropists celebrate them. But this space is different. This community built it themselves as a symbol of pride in their collective identity.

The center provides classes for kids to learn more about Iu Mien culture, history, and to preserve their language. Young college graduates return to staff the ongoing scholarship committee. At one point FII offered to provide funds to help the community buy a van to bring seniors to the center. The community accepted only a small portion of the funds and explained that the majority of the funds for the purchase had to come from the families to continue the pride that was developing within that community. Our funds were important, but making outside resources primary, they explained, would diminish the sense of community and self-determination.

Within a decade, the Iu Mien youth's expectation for their lives has changed; gangs are virtually gone and today the expectation for Iu Mien youth is to go to four year colleges. Other communities, be they Jewish, Irish, or Chinese, have also found that working together and having pride in your culture can create a shared positive expectation for each new generation.

Outsiders who recognize the success in the Iu Mien community tend to think that it was the community center, the classes, and the van that turned things around for the Iu Mien. The City of Oakland, and even my agency, tried to replicate this success, advocating for the building of more community centers and more programs where there were gang problems. But we could not replicate the real reason for the change in the Iu Mien community; the collective personal care and attention from parents and friends. The center and programs were but symbols of pride, of the love and caring that these parents had for their youth.

I began to realize that the communities that listened to my program staff might stop believing in themselves, much as Linda had said in chapter five: after a while *"if you consult programs often then you begin to be-*

lieve their way is the only way". She, along with May and the Iu Mien had to overcome or look past program solutions to truly succeed. It is not that programs or funding is not needed or important. It just can't be primary.

The story of the Iu Mien community in Oakland is not new. It is deeply rooted in the histories of marginalized and oppressed people throughout history. Cultural traditions have shown us that fostering the next generation, for instance, is not about buildings or services. Traditions, such as rites of passage, play a significant role in letting youth build self-confidence, find community wide support, and hold onto their identity in an often hostile or dismissive mainstream culture.

Although he didn't accept the invitation, my seventeen-year-old son was invited by a Native American tribe in Albuquerque to participate in a rite of passage for their youth; spending several days in the wilderness without food and water. Upon their return from the wild, the young person is celebrated with food and prayer by everyone in the tribe.

African American families in New Orleans who identify as part of the Mardi Gras tribes include their youth in making their costumes and competing in roles established specifically for their youth on Super Sunday, part of the Mardi Gras celebrations.

In the Latino community, there are quinceaneras where families come together to celebrate their fifteen-year-olds. The Jewish religion celebrates bar mitzvahs. All of these events are big deals with friends and family focusing on and honoring each of their children.

The Iu Mien parents donating $25 a month and celebrating their youth at the scholarships dinners, is a show of love and respect that surpasses the money. It is the demonstration of caring from other families, not the centers, that are important. These cultural celebrations and rituals cannot and should not be replaced by outside professional institutions. If a community of families is taking the initiative to build their own center or do a celebration for their youth, it would be best to match the funding families contribute and honor those efforts. This strategy is less costly, more effective, and sets an example for other communities to come together and to rebuild their sense of community.

Those communities have pride because they "own" their solutions. Just as the Iu Mien center has sustained and is now being copied in other parts of the country where there are substantial Mien communities, good ideas catch on. Self-defined paths are forged and can grow organically. These efforts can go to scale quickly. The *alternative* requires that we identify these positive deviant successes and support those wanting to follow similar paths.

People coming together don't have to be of the same ethnicity or religion. My personal community is made up of people who either work in the social service sector or care about the same issues and each other. One evening my niece and her two young boys showed up at my house. She had become depressed and relapsed into drugs. The next day, without telling us, she snuck out of the house and disappeared, leaving her five and seven-year-old boys with us. Overnight we became parents to not just our two kids but a total of four all around the same age. When friends, our community, found out, they offered to bring food, baby sit and even hold a fundraiser for us. Ours was a community of friends.

As a society, we need to learn that top-down solutions have never been the true instruments of change. While the Iu Mien parents were busy combating gang violence, I ran youth programs targeting gang members. The local police set up gang task forces and went to conferences and other cities to see what programs worked and tried to replicate them in the Bay Area. When I discussed these outside efforts with Kouichoy he just smiled and shook his head skeptically at the programs and all the money they cost.

"They wasted so much money," he commented with a smile because he knew I was one of the spenders. I knew my programs had limited impact on this issue, but I'm sure I told my funders that my programs were great, just as the police chief took credit for any incremental change that happened on his watch. On the other hand, no one outside of East Oakland ever heard about the collective action of Iu Mien parents. These parents, most on welfare, never got credit and certainly never received any of the grant funding that my organization did.

In the *Washington Post* panel mentioned earlier I also brought up that if we wanted to impact poverty we should learn from our history — from its successes and its failures. The idea was dismissed by the other panelists as they argued that "times have changed". It was becoming clear that if you want to come up with new solutions you shouldn't keep going back to the same "experts" because you will get the same answers and you will encounter the same limitations of success. *History and traditions give us many of the solutions we need.*

Do-it-yourself is our history

In the mid-1800s, thousands of Irish immigrants fleeing the potato famine in Ireland arrived in the United States only to face heavy discrimination. In response, they formed strong enclaves and helped one another into jobs and businesses. In 1851, Boston's Bernard "Barney" McGinniskin submitted an application to become the first Irish police officer in the

United States over protests so intense that he was fired, re-hired, and then fired again when a nativist political party took control of the city. Protesters argued that Irish-born Catholic police officers could not be trusted and that his position set "a dangerous precedent" because "Irishmen commit most of the city's crime and would receive special consideration from any of their own wearing the blue." Yet despite the public outrage, McGinniskin's hire started a path; by 1871 there were 45 officers of Irish background in Boston, and by the end of that century there were 100. Today the image of the Irish cop has been so thoroughly absorbed into mainstream popular culture, it's difficult to think this was once a source of public scandal. How did something once considered so extreme become so commonplace? This pattern is called positive deviance and will be explained in the next chapter.

Like their fellow newcomers to the U.S., Polish immigrants would go on to dominate an industry: for instance, the meatpacking factories particularly in Chicago. Arriving at a time when this industry was booming and other immigrant workers' failed strike had devolved into the 1886 Haymarket Riots, Polish laborers followed one another into meatpacking factories. There were no training programs or outreach initiatives to get men into these jobs. When employed workers referred a friend for a job they told them how to act, what to do, and how to dress. Employers thus continued to hire these already prepared workers.

The examples of the Irish and Polish are classic immigrant stories, the kind that Americans like to tell, boasting how they built a solid middle class. Yet the stories of African American communities, post-slavery, are also illustrative of this type of collective effort and success — and the ways that the U.S. allowed that hard-won prosperity to be deliberately destroyed.

In post-Civil War Oklahoma newly freed African Americans built over fifty all-black townships, each its own micro-economy since Blacks were largely excluded from doing business with white Americans. The Greenwood district of Tulsa, Oklahoma, was known as the *Black Wall Street,* with an economy so booming that residents formed their own schools, restaurants, and newspapers. Skills were learned and passed on. Financing was largely accomplished by pooling funds. Inspiration and support came from peers. Black professionals started emerging and within these supportive environments black professionals like lawyers and doctors were free to practice.

There were no government or nonprofit social service programs. Also, the increasing prosperity was not dependent on self-made individuals bootstrapping it. Those individuals would not have succeeded without being surrounded by a supportive environment. The most successful would reinvest in their own community. Sharing and mutuality was key. Friendships, family, as well as more collegial relationships were also necessary.

But in May 1921, when newspapers ran a fabricated story about a black man attempting to rape a white woman, a Ku Klux Klan-driven massacre decimated Greenwood. Overnight, more than 300 African Americans were murdered, over a thousand homes and 150 businesses were destroyed, and 9,000 Greenwood residents were left homeless. Black townships like Rosewood, Florida, met similar fates.

These stories illustrate not only the horror of racism in the United States, they also remind us that working together and helping one another is *not just an immigrant story*. Our natural history shows that success requires shared effort, and a larger society that allows, or even honors, communities to move up together. Service programs are supplements.

Despite the difference in outcomes, each group's story shares similar characteristics; a pride in one's community, a willingness to pool resources for the common good of the group, and leadership from those *within* a community, not those outside of it. The difference between these self-directed efforts and those of traditional service organizations is that in each of these instances families and cultural groups have exerted control from within a community context. Their actions fostered pride and self-respect, rather than detracted from it. And with some outside recognition, encouragement, and support, those historic traditions can again be the rule and not the exception.

These examples of self-generated success are reliant on a variety of relationships from loving, close personal relationships, to more collegial acquaintances. It isn't just about family or separately about village. Upward mobility dictates that we develop both, or what scholars classify as "strong ties" and "weak ties". Strong ties are those that must be nurtured and they thus provide ongoing reciprocal support. These are often family relationships but they also exist within close lasting friendships. My strong ties had been my mother, sister, and now close friends. For my mother, it had been Uncle Carlos in Mexico and her friends there.

Weak ties are extended networks, often relationships with co-workers, neighbors, or acquaintances. These ties don't require as much nurturing but they have value to both parties. These ties expose people to new ideas, new opportunities and new social networks. Business leaders are conscious of expanding weak ties to broaden their business or market connections. Now that I'm a part of the middle class I'm fully aware of the power of social networking.

The problem with the social services I ran is that while they extended our clients' weak ties, they also tended to undermine their strong ties, their closer more familial relationships, as we did with Myong. This is because these close relationships are already stressed by scarce resources as well as the negative images society has of those in poverty. We hurt those strong relationships because my staff had more resources in their control than our clients.

The graphic below depicts the roles of both strong and weak ties. Within strong ties there is generally a greater sense of trust and influence than with weak ties. But weak ties can provide new ideas, perspectives and new opportunities.

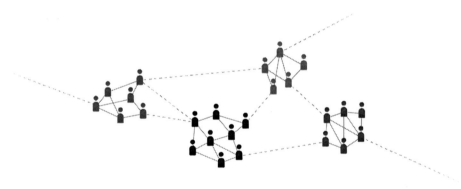

Strong Ties: In the stories I've provided the strong ties are relationships that last over time where there is a level of trust that is nurtured. Family often provides some of the strongest ties such as Richards girlfriend, May's family, my family, etc. Close friendships can also be long lasting connections of support. Strong ties are also demonstrated when assets are shared as occurs in some lending circles or the pooling of funds based on personal trust.

Weak Ties: Weak ties are relationships between members of different groups. They are utilized infrequently and therefore don't need as much ongoing nurturing. Business people will go to conferences or the golf club to meet new contacts or gain new insights. Weak ties can add a diversity of ideas and new opportunities as they bring together disparate modes of thought. The scaling or expansion of solutions or the paths described in this chapter are facilitated by weak ties, such as Iu Mien communities in other parts of the country that are now following the example of the Iu Mien in Oakland.

To be successful everyone needs the full spectrum of relationships — both strong and weak ties. *Getting ahead is truly a self-directed, but group effort.*

CHAPTER NINE

Positive Deviance and Epidemics
Instead of foam in the ocean, you get a wave

Ted Ngoy fled the killing fields of Cambodia at the end of the war in Vietnam, making it to California in the mid 1970s. He worked multiple jobs and eventually became manager of a Winchell's donut shop. In 1977, he opened his own donut shop, Christy's Donuts, in La Habra, California, and went on to help some friends open a few more shops. Word spread about this business model — a comfortable fit for recent immigrants whose English skills were still emerging — and they in turn helped others to open donut shops. A path to success was being forged[20]. Fifteen years later, Cambodian refugees came to own over eighty percent of the donut shops in California. Ted's role was part of a change process now described

---

20   Paths are formed through social networks such as the Vietnamese running manicure shops, or Afghan refugees being the primary cab drivers from Dulles airport, etc. But you see this in communities of the privileged where the children and friends of movie stars or financial moguls get opportunities and dominant positions in those fields.

as "positive deviance".

What is positive deviance? It is "an approach to behavioral and so-cial change based on the observation that in any community there are peo-ple whose uncommon but successful behaviors or strategies enable them to find better solutions to a problem than their peers, despite facing similar challenges." The people referenced here are not charismatic leaders, train-ers, teachers, or elected officials. Their socio-economic status or skills are not extraordinary and as such they are considered peers, similar in capa-bilities to those that they influence.

Positive deviants set a tangible example. They are the role models of what is possible. Often they help others to follow the path they have estab-lished. As peer role models, they are more effective than leaders, teachers, or trainers. My mother would take advice or believe the experiences of friends more than the advice from counselors who weren't facing similar circumstances. People used to share their experiences at the barber shops or beauty salons, just as the rich share at the country club.

Ted Ngoy started several donut shops and began to show others how to start similar shops. They didn't learn because of a business training program run by the local nonprofit. They saw and learned the specifics in real terms and then these new shop owners — the early adopters — helped cousins or friends. Once there were enough tangible examples within the Cambodian community the phenomenon reached a tipping point and spread quickly. Other Cambodians started intermediary business provid-ing distribution and equipment to serve the donut shops, creating even more jobs. Part-time jobs at the donut shops helped their children to go to college thus establishing college as part of the path for their youth. Donuts became a viable path of success for a sector of Cambodian refugees. Cambodians in Long Beach, California, started a multitude of auto repair shops in the same way and other self-defined positive deviant efforts happen in many low-income communities. We just need to look for them.

In the case of my bookkeeper, May's family, it is hard to locate the original positive deviants who carved their path but I am sure they existed. There are multiple paths in any community that are forged based on naturally developing, trusting relationships. Friendships and shared values seem to be the underpinnings of success. These affinities lead to the sharing of expertise as well as the pooling of capital if needed. These shared experiences change expectations and behaviors more effectively than programs. Funders would do well to focus on finding and meeting the families where they are in their lives, rather than spending millions on planning studies and theories of change.

A well-documented example of positive deviance began in 1990 in Vietnam. The Vietnamese government asked an international organization, *Save the Children*, to help fight malnutrition. Jerry Sternin led the effort. He recruited mothers from four different villages to weigh and document the diets of all the children. While it was clear after looking at the data that the traditional norms or diets were leaving the children malnourished, the solution was not clear. Western diets and norms wouldn't work here given the difference in income and foods available. They asked local mothers if they knew of any kids who were heavier and healthier than most. They found that there were a small number of well-nourished children in each of the villages and began to investigate. First, they eliminated the outliers who might be better off because of a connection to a government official who could get them more or better food, etc. They needed to find the otherwise typical families with healthier children and they then compared what differences existed from the norm. Upon interviewing the positive deviant families about how they were feeding their children they could not pin point a specific difference from the rest of the villagers. Their next step was to visit the homes to observe and then discovered differences that the families had failed to describe, likely because they took those behaviors for granted.

Researchers found that the positive deviant families were adding tiny bits of shrimp or snail to the meals and that their children ate several times a day rather than just twice a day as most families did. Armed with this information their first impulse was to set up classes, train teachers and create educational materials for villagers, but their budget was too limited. Instead, they turned to the positive deviant families and asked if they would cook together with other village families.

The peer exchange worked. Since peer families were now teaching their techniques to their neighbors it was clear that the solution came from and was owned by the village residents themselves. That the solution worked in their cultural context meant that there was a much better chance that the new behaviors would sustain after Save the Children left Vietnam. I felt that Myong, in a previous story, turning to her friends' for support, also illustrated this dynamic.

Besides the idea being homegrown, there were other elements that also helped that positive deviant behavior to spread. Save the Children and the government documented the changes in weight and nutritional health of the subject children and shared that information with villagers all over Vietnam. As the word spread from one friend to another, from one village to another, the data validated these efforts. That is the same role played by FII in our *alternative* model; the role of validator and facilitator, not leader, for the sharing of home grown solutions.

Over the next seven years in Vietnam over fifty thousand children were positively impacted as old behaviors began to change. The cost was minimal and the solution more sustainable than if it had been developed by outsiders and applied through leaders, trainers, or teachers.

We all are more inclined to listen to a trusted peer when trying something new. This is more fully documented in the book, *The Speed of Trust*. This takes us back to the importance of strong ties. While we may also listen to a social worker or a teacher, developing new habits or taking new action is easier and spreads more quickly, if you see a peer, someone like you, taking on the new behavior or sharing it.

Sternin recalled that one of the more senior volunteers shared an old saying which translated from Vietnamese was roughly "A thousand hearings is not worth one seeing, and a thousand seeings is not worth one doing."

Peer exchange brings out other helpful human qualities.

FOMO and mutuality

If some of your peers are sharing on Facebook then you are more likely to join. If a peer of yours succeeds, you may be inspired or even become jealous, wanting to also succeed. Any of these human reactions about peers can begin a process of change. Fear-of-missing-out (FOMO) comes into play and keeping up with the Jones's is natural. Behavioral reinforcement is made more powerful if those actions emerge naturally from your community.

Outside programs will often try to artificially *create* a sense of community by picking and grouping the families themselves, rather than recognizing existing relationships. When I ran social service programs I felt group efforts were important so my staff would bring families from my training or my housing programs together in groups. But those group relationships didn't sustain without my staff providing the framework or support. Some programs seek this dependent relationship since it becomes a justification for funding. But dependency does not lead to sustainability. From my experience it is clear that the groups my staff formed tended to fall away when our program or its funding was cut.

A test of the durability of a community movement is whether it continues without the paid professionals to guide it. This lesson was reinforced for me when my friend Kouichoy, from the Iu Mien community, refused funds to pay his volunteers.

"If I pay some," he told me, "then the others will stop coming up with their own ideas and volunteering." Personal commitment is worth much more than money. I learned so much from Kouichoy, Michelle and the Iu Mien community.

The crucial role of early adopters

One of the U.S.'s strongest cultural biases is also a huge hindrance to bringing about fundamental social change: *individualism.* We celebrate individuality and individual leaders to the point that it diminishes the role of friends, extended family, and community. Individuals — Martin Luther King Jr., Bill Gates, Cesar Chavez, or the Mayor, the President — are often credited as the initiators or centers of change. No one would argue that these leaders don't play an important role in spreading change but what is not recognized are the many ordinary people who were brave enough to test a new product, start a protest, or change behavior.

It is the combination of the positive deviants and early adopters, *backed* by leaders, which brings about change. Too often the glorification of the more charismatic leader diminishes the role of the early adopters — the ordinary people who are crucial to large scale change. There are tons of new and innovative ideas introduced every day but if there are no regular folks taking a chance on them, trying and testing them, then the ideas are unlikely to go anywhere.

At a meeting of a group made up of recipients of the MacArthur "Genius" Fellowship[21], we felt exceptionally lucky to win this prestigious award and be considered leaders in our field. But we were fully aware that so many others had played a role and weren't recognized.

Though I was honored with a MacArthur Fellowship, what I know is that those that I learn from, the role models I follow, are the Iu Mien families and Kouichoy, the Mardi Gras tribes, the many families whose stories are in this book, and of course my mother and sister. All go unrecognized. I can spread their ideas, but I didn't develop them.

One of the other MacArthur recipients recounted a story of the period in the civil rights movement when she was a member of SNCC, the Student Nonviolent Coordinating Committee. As an organization, it had moved away from having one designated leader and made decisions by consensus as a group. After a mob of Ku Klux Klan members attacked integrated groups of bus passengers, she was among some SNCC members

---

21   The MacArthur Fellows Program, sometimes called the "genius grant" is a prize awarded annually by the John D. and Catherine T. MacArthur Foundation to individuals working in a wide variety of fields who have shown extraordinary originality or dedication in their pursuits. It is considered to be one of the most prestigious awards for individuals in the United States. I was awarded in October of 2012.

who joined the Freedom Rides[22] happening in the deep South. On her first night in Mississippi they huddled together in a shack on the outskirts of town. Later, after night fall, they heard rustling outside and whispers of men moving around the house. Finally, getting up their courage they opened the door and looked out to find a number of black men with rifles surrounding their place. When the men noticed them looking somewhat scared, they apologized.

"We are sorry if we woke you" they explained, "but you know that you are in danger so some of us just thought we would sit out here in case there was trouble. Just get some sleep. We will be here." She went on to say that while charismatic leaders were inspiring and important, when her life was on the line, the self-initiated leadership shown by those ordinary men meant so much more.

What is ignored in the social service sector is the self-organization which happens because of self-interest. In this case, the self-interest was not individual but for the good of their community. These initiatives should be recognized and honored by society. Ordinary citizens don't put their life on the line if it isn't important. Rather than the focus on individual leaders, even like myself, the non-profit sector needs to learn to recognize, honor, and support actions the early adopters take because these self-interested group actions have the best chance of catching on with other ordinary people and thus reach a tipping point.

---

22   The Freedom Rides were started in May of 1961 by a group of 13 African-American and white civil rights activists to challenge the non-enforcement of a Supreme Court decision which ruled that segregated public buses were unconstitutional. The riders of these buses encountered tremendous violence from white protestors.

Going to scale by reaching a Tipping Point

Another way of explaining the role of early adopters, those ordinary but adventurous folks, is to imagine you come up with a great idea, maybe a game for losing weight. You go to a park to announce it. Standing on the opposite side of a fence is the audience you want. You yell out and explain your idea to those sitting on the other side of the fence. It is rare that everyone will then stand up, climb the fence and adopt the new idea. More likely one or two will become curious enough to venture to your side and a few of their friends, based on trust, will follow. After trying it out, if they like your idea, they will stay on your side of the fence.

These are the early adopters — folks that are brave enough to consider a new behavior. Most people are hesitant and they wait. Only after these early adopters have tested and validated the idea will the others follow and only then can you reach a tipping point when adoption spreads quickly. The idea or the leader is not the trend setter. While charismatic leaders can help market the idea, what matters are those early adopters who moved to your side of the fence. *The early adopters are the trend setters.*

There have been a lot of studies about how new ideas spread. How did Facebook or even certain fashions become popular or the accepted norm? *Diffusion of innovation theory* proposes that to gain prominence an idea has to have some early adopters before it can reach a critical mass and become widely accepted. There is generally an innovator, the positive deviant, such as Ted Ngoy and his donut shop. Then there are the early adopters, the first group of youngsters from the Iu Mien community to go to college or Ted's friends in Los Angeles. But there is generally a period of time, the chasm, when you don't know if the tipping point will be reached. You don't know if the idea is any good. But as small actions by early adopters accumulate there comes a point where the idea becomes acceptable and change scales, reaching large numbers very quickly. Expectations or tastes are then more fundamentally changed and can sustain for extended periods.

The following chart depicts this well researched phenomenon.

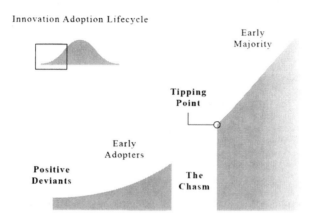

Businesses are constantly selling their ideas but they carefully track if the idea is being adopted. If there aren't enough early adopters they drop the idea or product. *Fail fast* is now a catch phrase, at least within the tech industry. But in the nonprofit or social service sector even bad ideas can survive as long as there are funders willing to provide funds. Programs don't fail fast and there is very little effort to see the preferences of the recipients or if the families might have better solutions. People showing up for services is often mistaken as demand rather than the result of families lacking choices. But solutions can exist within the communities themselves, as Save the Children found in Vietnam. These naturally occurring solutions should be presented as options for those we want to help.

Change does not happen evenly or in a linear fashion. Change requires an accumulation of small acts which at some point reach a critical mass, a tipping or turning point. In his book, *Tipping Point,* Malcolm Gladwell outlined many of the underlying qualities that can lead to tipping points. Lots of small actions such as those taken by the villagers in Vietnam cooking together may not look like much on their own but when self-organizing hits a tipping point, change can happen very quickly. This type of change is viral, like an epidemic, and epidemics scale up much faster than policies or programs.

This is a critical point because one of the criticisms aimed at FII's approach of starting with small groups of families is that it can't grow to a scale that can slow or stop the cycle of poverty. Those interested in large scale social change try to come up with a big top-down idea or policy to bring about change, *not* trusting that small, naturally occurring actions, can scale, often more quickly because they are based in *trust*[23]. Yet this process of small-to-large is how communities historically have thrived. Local actions such as farmer's markets are proliferating, for example, and the politician's role should be to facilitate, not lead, that expansion. If we want change in our low-income communities and we want those residents to protect or sustain that change, then we have to look at *their* small actions, the thousands or millions of small initiatives they take to make their lives better. Humanity is a big ocean. *Instead of foam in the ocean, you get a wave!*

In 2011, FII learned that there were three groups of friends in San Francisco that had started traditional lending circles. Lending circles have a long history and have been used within communities to self-finance.

---

23 Trust accelerates change. One reference is the book, "The Speed of Trust".

Lending circles vary greatly in how they are structured, but essentially a group of families or friends commit to putting in any amount, say $50 a month, into a common pool, then they take turns borrowing the entire pool. Some use the funds to buy a car, pay for school, or even pay taxes. Each participant chooses how to spend the funds. This type of communal saving and lending requires a certain amount of trust between participants, but that mutual accountability reinforces and strengthens close relationships. People start to help one another in other ways, even just providing emotional support.

When FII families living in East Boston heard of the three lending circles in San Francisco they said, "We used to do that in our home country, Colombia." A few of them started lending circles and word spread in Boston. Once the viability of the model was proven, even families that had never been exposed to group saving began circles. The idea accelerated and in four years the phenomenon grew from three circles who pooled about $3,000 annually, to over seventy lending circles pooling over $1.7 million dollars. Businesses and jobs are created, kids go to college and health problems are addressed.

Looking for positive deviance and early adopters within communities is more complex than our typical narrative of the lone, charismatic leader, teacher, or even a program. To shift our thinking requires us to recognize that the everyday initiative of the many plays a more critical role than the grand gestures of those we designate as heroes. Ted Ngoy was not a charismatic leader or teacher. Ultimately, he lost his fortune gambling and ended up homeless on the porch of one of the families that he had helped to start a donut shop. The men that put their lives on the line to protect not just my friend, but all the Freedom Riders, will never be recognized but we need to grasp and honor their importance even as we honor those individuals who we designate as heroes. To commemorate most wars we see statues of the generals, but I particularly appreciate the Vietnam War Memorial in Washington, DC, that does a wonderful job of honoring the ordinary soldiers by listing the names of all that fell in that conflict. *Change requires tribute to the ordinary.*

CHAPTER TEN

Modeling the Alternative
The Basics of the Family Independence Initiative

To impact the over 100 million people who are economically part of the bottom 2/5ths of our population, the *alternative* cannot be a program or be institutionalized. You can't "program" that many people out of the cycle of poverty. There is no "vaccine". It must be a natural process that promotes the positive aspects of human nature. The change process must, at its core, be natural and organic, even if it is helped by leaders and institutions. It must support the characteristics that Daniel Pink identified: the "deep human need to direct our own lives, to learn and create new things, and to do better by ourselves and our world." It must support collective efforts such as the mutuality that led African Americans after slavery to build townships. It must allow for the diversity of humanity to be preserved and allowed to grow organically. Efforts to institutionalize informal efforts too often hinder their natural growth.

The *alternative* is likely to make those that seek nicely packaged approaches uncomfortable. Human processes are messy, even chaotic. But there are patterns that emerge from that seeming chaos and we need to look at the patterns that make it a better world for all of us. The world is diverse and we should always look for, and gravitate to, the positive aspects of that beautiful diversity we call humanity. The private sector accommodates itself to the diversity of the market place and so should the social service sector. The proposed *alternative* is shaped by those directly participating and thus will work in most any community. These are some of the characteristics that the *alternative* incorporates and were described in previous chapters:

- **Control**: Since we don't have a stagnant, passive underclass, those in control of outside resources must step aside so that the families and their communities can lead their own change. What I have learned is that trusting the families to take the lead surfaces both positive deviants and early adopters. Those in the social service sector are mostly wonderful, well-intentioned people, but they must realize that the control their social status gives them over ideas and resources, diminishes the leadership of family and community.
- **Choices**: What appear to be bad decisions by families are most often due to a lack of choices. Families deserve a wide range of choices which those that are more privileged take for granted. This is not a call for vouchers. We don't give vouchers as benefits to the rich. Since most choice comes to those with money, then one theme of the proposed *alternative* is to match the funds that families themselves commit, so they can afford the choices normally open to only the

privileged.

- **Community**: History has shown us that getting out of poverty requires more than individual effort; it requires collective action, it's a group effort. We must honor and support families who come together locally and virtually, to learn and help one another. Today's technology can play a role and begin to connect people across the country and across the world, as well as giving everyone access to the same information.

FII was not set up to be the institution or program that would save everyone. It was set up to demonstrate this new "bottom up" approach. It shows that getting professional helpers out of the way leads to better outcomes. Some of the struggles and successes of modeling this new approach follow.

*

After I told Jerry Brown of my idea for the Family Independence Initiative, he threw his considerable weight behind my project. I got some initial funding and FII started in 2001. With FII I was trying to design a system that would have let my mother keep her pride and that would have been willing to invest in her talents and demonstrated hard work. It was set up to help ordinary families, not the exceptions. The data I wanted to collect lay in the stories of families like my own; their ideas, their success and failures and how the success of positive deviants could spread. Could the families take their small wins, gain early adopters and ultimately change the expectations and lives of entire communities as the Iu Mien and others have done?

The Family Independence Initiative was set up to recognize the initiative of the families themselves and to develop a way that makes resources, connections, and money, available to them based on the actions they take *of their own volition*. Since we would be learning and adjusting based on the actions the families take, FII was not a fixed program. Over the years it has evolved locally and will continue to evolve or adjust to each new community and the pattern of actions that emerge from those who are participating.

In its design and evolution I tried to leave behind the typical "social service" thinking; the theories of change and fixed program guidelines that had driven my last twenty years of work. I promised myself to design what we did based on the common sense I used to run my own life every day. If it didn't make sense to a middle-income family, then it didn't make sense.

After running traditional social service programs for two decades I was very aware that transforming traditional expectations on both the staff and family side was not going to be easy. To get the true stories and data of the capability of low-income families, two things needed to happen.

First, we had to assure that our staff would step back and trust families to lead their own change. Staff needed to understand that its role was simply to validate the families as the experts of their own lives, much as Save the Children did in Vietnam, and to verify the data and stories provided by the families about what they did for themselves and for others.

And secondly, we had to convince the participating families that they had to take action and lead their own change; that they shouldn't wait for direction from outsiders, and that they, not FII staff, had to be the primary supports for each other.

The two elements we hoped to see emerge were that families would take *control* as well as strengthen their sense of *community*.

Getting staff to back off from helping

Since FII was incorporated as a nonprofit it was perceived to be just another social service agency. Given this initial perception, one of the most difficult tasks was to get FII staff to NOT be helpful to participating families, so that they would take control in how they would improve their own lives. After my experience running social services I was very aware that just the social status of being a paid staffer in FII gave my staff implicit power over our clients. I had to ensure that my staff would relinquish that power. FII staff was warned that if they did provide help or counsel to participants, they would be fired. To date four staff members have been fired for being helpful!

Wandy Peguero, the staff liaison to some of the Boston families struggled with this concept. The liaison's role was to only verify the data reported by families and capture the stories behind the data. He wrote:

When I joined FII-Boston I was really skeptical of this work. The idea that a non-profit organization is not allowed to "help" was a foreign language to me. Six months into my time with FII I was approached by a family member who asked me to translate a letter, from English to Spanish. I knew that as a liaison I was not supposed to do translation, but my traditional non-profit experience kicked in and I helped.

This was my first test, and I failed. Three weeks later that same family approached me with the same request. I quickly tried to put my FII game face on but in the end I translated the letter once more. After the second translation, I thought to myself, this is exactly what FII doesn't want, for families to rely on "professional" help, but to rely on their social connections. The third time came around, and this time I asked the family if she had asked anyone else to translate the letter. She said "no, because I am counting on you", and it hit me I had completely failed at what FII was trying to prove. I explained to the family FII's model and asked that she reach out to a member of her group or her community for support with the translation.

She totally agreed with FII's model and has never asked me to translate another letter. After that a friend did the translations and they became closer. This experience has repeated itself many, many times on issues big and small. Rebuilding mutuality and pride in community means my stepping back.

Paola Hernandez, a liaison in San Francisco wrote that it was also a difficult transition for her:

There is no single moment I can pinpoint, but an experience that really impacted my thinking was with Ida. She is a single mother, well over 50 years old, who is raising a teenage son. She's also an immigrant who speaks only Spanish and works a blue-collar job to make ends meet. When told that an email was required to stay in FII, Ida's first question was, "What's an email?"

It would've been very easy for me to just create an email for her, but after explaining what email is, I left it at that. A few weeks later I met with Ida. Beaming with pride, she told me she'd created an email account for herself. I saw that as a key moment for Ida and for me. I saw that when she accomplished a goal without my help — regardless of how small the goal — it made a substantial change in her demeanor. Ida became more confident in her own abilities. She started to see in herself what FII sees in all our families: She is capable of leading her family on its own path toward success. That first accomplishment was only the beginning. Now she is involved in a lending circle, helps to finance her son's education, and is pushing herself to learn as much as she can.

What I've seen time and time again is that after a family accomplishes the very first goal they have set for themselves, the family changes. Their disposition changes, their level of assurance changes, and even their approach changes.

I've had the honor of getting to know many other families who have proven that they have superior knowledge to mine about so many things, like surviving in the worst neighborhoods in America. Each of them is just as driven by determination as the last, and each has innovative ideas that obliterate the discrimination they are challenged with daily. But one fact remains constant: When families faithfully believe in themselves, anything is possible. During my years with FII, I've seen that allowing families to successfully achieve their first goal independently is a crucial point that reveals this significant truth to us — helping really doesn't help.

Getting families to take the lead

Getting staff to step back didn't ensure that the families would automatically step up. In our first years some families thought we were a scam of some kind since we wanted to know so much about their lives. Things have changed and now enrolled families explain the purpose to new families and as peers their explanations are more readily accepted. When we first started FII in 2001, we only enrolled families in groups of friends that they had recruited themselves. We wanted the families to have a sense of power that comes from being in a group of like-minded friends. From FII they would get a computer and they would need to enter what they did or accomplished each month to improve their lives; we would pay them a nominal amount (now about $50 per report they submit) for their time once our staff verified what they entered into our online journaling system.

The first thing they heard when enrolled was that they would be the leaders of their own change. Our staff was only there to observe and verify what they entered online, not to help. The FII families would have to turn to one another for support. At the initial orientation they would hear something like this:

We are not here to help you. We want you to help us. Your liaison sitting back there is not allowed to give you any direction or advice. After all, you are the experts of your own lives, of your own kids, so we are here to learn from you.

You also need to know that you are part of a much bigger project. Most of our country thinks that you are not the experts of your family or lives. The reality is that you are not trusted just because you are poor. This is your chance to prove everyone wrong. This is your chance to change your life your way. If you ever wanted to improve your life this is the time to do it. We will pay you for the time it takes you to give us the data and stories about how you change your life.

We want to learn from you — what works and what doesn't that you try. But if this is not time for change for you, then it is better that you don't join FII, because if you do nothing, then we learn nothing, and if we learn nothing, you will earn nothing. That's all there is to it. If you want to join us in changing the country, then stick around.

Some of the groups understood the approach right away and did not try to get advice from staff. Others struggled, waiting or even asking for direction from the staff liaison assigned to each group. We enrolled one group of Samoan families living in public housing in San Francisco. They assumed we were like any other program and since we wouldn't tell them what we wanted them to do they went onto our web site. They saw that quite a few FII families before them had bought homes, so at a meeting I attended they asked, "So do you want us to buy homes? Is that it? Really, what do you expect us to do in this program?" It took them a while to believe we were there to learn from them.

But one of the most dramatic ways we made it clear that families were leading the way was to fire staff that tried to give them advice or support.

One of our staff liaisons, Mathew, tried to hide that he was helping some of the families. We discovered it because he was paid by the hours he spent with the families and his hours kept going up. Also, many of the families he worked with had not established the required email accounts. It turned out that he felt sorry for some of the families who had never used a computer and so he acted as the information conduit, phoning them, so that they didn't have to struggle with learning to email. He was also helping some families to do their monthly journals.

We confronted him, explaining that we didn't feel he trusted the resourcefulness of families enough and so we were letting him go. He countered that he felt bad that so many families were struggling with their computers. He was well-intended, but didn't understand that his pity was actually disempowering the very people he cared about. This is such a hard idea for very compassionate people to absorb.

When we told the families that he was to be fired some of the families protested and wanted to meet with me. The protesting families came prepared to argue that they were not dependent on him but they just wanted a little help, much as they had gotten in other programs. In response, I showed them a short video of television clips where commentators and even presidential candidates, portrayed families like theirs as lazy or in the case of more liberal pundits, saying that the families needed professionals like Matthew or they couldn't get ahead.

"Even if you don't feel like you are dependent on Matt, American society doesn't believe that you can do all you do without him. They will give credit to Mathew's skills, not your skills, for any progress you make. Your role is to help us break those stereotypes of you and your friends." Finally, some of the families nodded.

"Also," I continued, "your liaisons are charging us for the time they spend helping you, taking away money that we could give to you for doing it yourself or helping others." I explained that the two part-time liaisons were costing FII about $100,000 for salary, benefits and office support.

"Wouldn't it be better if some of that money went to you as scholarships or awards?" The families never imagined that instead of paying staff, the money could go to them for helping themselves and each other. The protest was dying down when someone in the back of the room stood up and asked.

"Some of us have never had a computer or an email! How are we supposed to do this?" Then Dolores, the teen daughter of one of the families stood up and turned to the families behind her "I'll help you!" she offered, "I'll help all of you!"

"Wouldn't it be better if FII gave her some scholarship money instead of me paying staff?" I added. "You have the experts among you. I would rather pay all of you rather than Mathew."

The protest dissipated and the families somehow found friends to help. It wasn't very hard to promote the rebuilding of mutuality and the recognition that there were those within their community that were as capable as my staff.

My confidence in letting Matt go and dealing with the protest came from an experience when I first started FII. I have many confessions to make but my first is to confess that in the beginning, like Matt, I underestimated what families could do for themselves and one another.

My idea of giving each FII family a computer was an inexpensive way of getting monthly longitudinal data from them. At the same time, I knew that many of the enrolled families had never used a computer. I initially formed a technology committee to design training for the families. I was on a trip when the first set of computers arrived and the families came to our offices to get the computers and training. When I returned from my trip I asked the staff how it went.

"It was a mess," was the reply. "The trainer just wasn't able to answer all the questions and everyone got frustrated. Then we didn't have any hand carts for the families to carry the computers to their cars — if they even had a car!"

"So are any of the families online yet?" I asked somewhat concerned.

"Oh, they are all online," was the reply. "One seventeen-year -old that came with her mother volunteered to help everyone set things up and then they all helped one another carry the computers downstairs. The ones with cars helped the ones without cars and it all worked out." Their sense of community and mutuality was inadvertently enhanced.

I disbanded the technology committee. We no longer try to solve problems. We just ask the families to do it themselves. As examples of mutuality have grown, what we have found is that every time my staff has stepped back, the families have stepped up and their solutions are much more relevant to their circumstance or culture than ours could ever be.

Sometimes it takes patience on our side. One of my first liaisons complained to me that while one of the groups had a lot of potential, she didn't feel they were doing enough. "Can I say something to them?" My reply was "No, have patience. You aren't trusting them enough". This is the group whose average income ultimately jumped 37 percent within two years. From the outside we make assumptions that life is more linear or logical than it is. I remember how complex life was for my mother and why she couldn't follow up on some opportunities that seemed obvious to others. Those choices have to be left to the family.

My biggest lesson about community role models, about positive deviants, happened seven months into the FII project in Oakland. We had enrolled five families who were refugees from the war in El Salvador. Javier and his wife Maria were among them and they were typically very quiet in their monthly meetings.

Then at one of the meetings Javier announced, "Vamos a comprar una casa!" or we're going to buy a house! For about seven months homeownership had never come up as a goal. Instead the stated goals from all the families in this group had been to take care of their health, assure their kids did well in school, and send money back to relatives in their home village in El Salvador. My staff reported this new goal to me with some surprise since this family rarely spoke up and didn't appear to be risk takers — and they had no savings!

When I spoke with the couple in my elementary Spanish they told me that a Spanish-speaking real estate agent assured them he could help them buy the house at the end of the street. They found friends to lend them money for the inspections and deposits — but my staff reported that they suspected the agent was a predatory lender. They asked if they could advice the family or get them to go to financial training workshops. I refused. I had promised Mayor Brown that my staff would not interfere and so we would have to step back and just observe. My staff was not happy.

Sure enough, since the agent made his money upon closing, he did get them the house. But he added mortgage insurance so that their monthly payment ended up being 65 percent of Javier and Maria's income. My staff was truly upset with me for not letting them advise the family. I also felt bad. It was clear that the family would lose the house.

But the situation carried some surprising lessons. Somewhere along the way, Javier and Maria recognized that they had gotten in over their head and made sure there was a refinance clause in their financing papers. After closing on the house, they called on friends again, who then descended on the house, re-tiled, re-landscaped, and re-painted it. Their efforts increased the assessed valuation of the house. Six months later they refinanced and got their payments down to about 40 percent of their income. And with this community of friends surrounding them, it was clear they would not lose the house. In fact, they still have the house!

The next lesson came two months after Javier and his wife stabilized the financing of their house. Our data system, which allows us to see the savings level of all participants, showed a sudden surge in savings for all of the families in that cohort. Before, they had all sent any savings they accumulated back to El Salvador — referred to as remittances — something many immigrants do. At the next monthly meeting I asked the other families in that cohort why they were suddenly saving so much.

They all answered, "Well, if Javier and Maria can get a house, we can get one too!" It turned out that Javier and Maria were the positive deviants. Though living under the same circumstances as their peers, they had done something unusually successful. Within eighteen months of that meeting *all* the other four families in this group owned homes in the United States! These early adopters did not make the mistake of using Javier and Maria's broker.

And there was one more lesson which goes back to the idea of the tipping point. It seemed that most of the families in the broader Salvadoran refugee community felt it would be impossible to build assets in the United States. That is why they sent all their savings back to their villages. When others heard not only about Javier and Maria, but also about the other families in their group, the early adopters, it changed the expectations and goals of many others in that refugee community. Many began to save and pool their money to buy homes. There had been a ripple effect as expectations changed and a new path was forged.

In December of 2016, fifteen years after Javier and Maria bought their home, I did a presentation at Stanford University and shared this story. After the speech, a young Salvadoran man walked up to me.

"You know, my mother was one of those that heard of the families in FII buying homes and so our family also decided to buy a house. It is the equity from that house that we used to get me through Stanford. Thank you so much!"

That moment was probably one of the most gratifying for me even though I wasn't the one who led the change. *My role had been to step back and trust.*

You can't really change a country as the old saying goes, one person at a time. Success comes when expectations are changed within an entire community and that requires early adopters, not just an individual example, a charismatic leader, or just the positive deviant. What is best is to do what Sternin did in Vietnam; encourage and support peers to educate and share their knowledge and resources. Towards this end FII began to provide matching funds to those that wanted to follow the new path that was being forged. Our task was to accelerate the creation of early adopters to see if we could reach a tipping point. We did not intervene to create the idea, but instead waited for homegrown ideas to emerge and to see if others followed. It is only at this stage that we feel outside support can help to scale change.

When I told Javier and Maria's story to colleagues, some asked, "but what if the others had used that same crooked lender?" It is a bit of a shocking question. It indicates how low our expectations are of people that are poor, even by the well-intended. Javier and his wife realized at some point that he was a scam artist but they were too far into the deal before he showed his true colors. Making mistakes with money is not isolated to the poor. Many rich, and supposedly financially savvy families, lost life savings to investment scammer "Bernie" Madoff, for example. The solution that Javier and Maria came up with to improve the value of the property with the help of friends and then to refinance could not have been designed by my staff. It was like the old-fashioned community barn-raisings and it illustrates just how capable their community was, even in the face of scarcity and mistakes.

The biggest lost opportunity for change, however, came from the group of friends that enrolled in Oakland who were largely African American. When they first enrolled the average income hovered around poverty level but then, influenced by one another, each family began progressing. This group began organizing themselves in the most isolated neighborhood of West Oakland, the *Village Bottoms*. They had a vision of developing their own "Chinatown"; a strip of shops and clubs, a jazz district, that would revitalize the area and be a point of pride for the black community. They started a coffee shop, art gallery, small grocery store and tilapia farm. At one point the families from that area had purchased at least ten homes or properties, as well as a former garage which was repurposed to become a community center.

I was especially impressed by this center called The Black New World. Renovated by volunteers, it was used to host hip-hop classes for youth and to conduct performances at night. Although that neighborhood had a myriad of nonprofit and government services, this self-made center is where kids went to stay off the street. This center evoked pride because it was set up and led by residents.

Over the previous 20 years the city and private foundations had committed millions of dollars to establish community centers in that area.

They all failed. Standing in front of Black New World, members from that group pointed to the vacant building at the end of the street, "That was the last screw up". The professionally run programs and the nicely decorated venues did not attract as much attention from residents as this homegrown center.

As a member of the board of a large foundation, the California Endowment, I led a tour of this area for the board and staff. I hoped they could see the potential of this volunteer initiative and that they would provide grants to support those efforts. One board member, however, voiced concern that the effort was not professionally led and therefore would ultimately fail. This came up even after hearing and seeing how all the well-funded professional efforts had failed, and that the Iu Mien continued to voluntarily support the center they voluntarily built. Ultimately there was no support from this or other foundations. In a short video shown at a conference, one of the residents stated something like:

> Every foundation and every new Mayor comes here [the Village Bottoms area] with their ideas and they have all failed. These outside do-gooders come into our hood with a missionary mentality. Like somebody like Tarzan. The whole giving system needs to be dismantled and reborn so that it rewards self-determination.

Over my 35 years in social service work in Oakland I have seen every major program, funder, or government designed initiative come into the West Oakland area and fall flat on its face. Millions upon millions have been spent. If the professionals failed, then why not trust the residents themselves for once? But the city and foundations refused to support any of the West Oakland families' grassroots initiative and the Black New World failed because it couldn't raise the funds to retrofit the building for earthquakes, as called by the city building department.

While there were setbacks in gaining support from foundations and government, I was amazed by the accomplishments of those first families whose efforts were documented by FII. Within two years the income of the group of friends who were primarily African American increased an average of 37 percent, for the Salvadoran refugees, their income increase was 23 percent, and the average income of the Asian Iu Mien group was 18 percent. Savings went up, debt went down, and each group developed its own patterns as they helped and modeled for one another.

The Iu Mien families, who had been primarily on welfare, had the lowest income increase of the first participants in FII. But they made huge progress in redirecting their teens from gangs to college. This community's self-defined goal was to create a new path for their youth and they didn't focus on personal income as a measure of success.

The Latino refugee group, with Javier and Maria, all bought homes and changed expectations for others regarding the possibility of building assets in this country.

The group primarily made up of African American families started the most businesses, owned the most property, and worked to make their neighborhood safer as well as to rebuild pride in their culture.

After Oakland, FII started projects in Hawaii, San Francisco, Boston and Detroit and over the next decade we saw consistency in the progress families made within two years in FII's empowering environment.

	Oakland (Year) 24 Months	Hawaii 20 Months	San Francisco 24 Months	Boston 24 Months	Detroit 15 Months
Income Avg. Increase	26%	18%	21%	24%	23%
Savings Avg. Increase	144%	377%	215%	250%	130%
% of Families with Side Businesses	25%	12%	20%	28%	30%
% of Kids with Grades/Attend Up	70%	60%	72%	80%	70%

Although the progress indicated by traditional measures of success such as income has been significant, what is the most encouraging is the increased confidence and sense of control I've seen in families who formerly felt discouraged or disempowered by our society. Mutuality and community are the vital key ingredients to success. Yet, if you think that FII is the silver bullet that we have searched for over the last fifty-year war on poverty, then you have missed the point. FII is there to demonstrate that if our society would trust families to make their own decisions, and then back the actions those families take, we could have large scale success. It takes more than a few programs. Seeing people as contributors and investing in their initiative by banks, philanthropists, businesses, and government is what can grow our economy and close the income and wealth gap. Our society provides that for the rich. Common sense should now tell us that a *hands-off, trusting, encouraging environment is the nectar of success for our lower income populations.*

CHAPTER ELEVEN

The Right (data) Stuff
The thousand cars doing the right thing

If the information you get represents the exception rather than the rule, you won't understand what's real. In 2015, I had the opportunity to hear jazz bassist Victor Wooten play at a club in my hometown, Oakland, California. His performance had the entire audience singing and clapping. Before he began his last piece, he said something along the lines of;

I travel all around the world and I meet wonderful people like you everywhere. But when you read the newspapers you read about the bad stuff, the bad people. That is what makes news. That is what people pay attention to. It makes the world seem like a bad place. We don't pay enough attention to the good stuff, to the people that don't cross the street as they walk towards me. When someone cut me off on the freeway in Oakland I heard "well that's Oakland for you!" But what about the other thousand cars passing by doing the right thing?

Victor's comments stayed with me. His words resonated because most of my social service colleagues are focused on what's wrong in the communities we serve. We are constantly being told by some new study that living with scarcity means that low-income families can't make good decisions, or that low-income parents don't say enough words to their children to bolster literacy skills. After thirty-five years of working in the social sector I have observed that to stay "fresh" we invent new negative stereotypes to ascribe to "the poor." Yet there are positive actions and good decisions taking place every day across this country that stay invisible and so are not honored. We need to shift the studies and information we listen to and see the other side.

At an event organized by FII families in Boston, they shared the strides they were making working together with friends and family. At the end of the night, Torli Krua approached me and said, "You have to start an FII in my home country, Liberia, and other African countries. When people hear about Africa all they hear is about wars, disease, hunger and helpless people. They never hear how my people survive all that; how they build, help, and love each other."

The point Victor and Torli were both making is that society's perception of entire populations is often based on the negative things that are the exception, rather than the rule. We're looking at people through the wrong lens. We hear distorted perceptions every day in conversations about Muslims, Black Americans, or poor families in our country. Our first step in changing the way this country invests in working families is to see what Victor Wooten saw that night on the freeway — *the thousands doing the right thing.*

In designing what data to collect in FII, I interviewed families and realized that to understand the complexity of their lives I had to capture a wide range of information. I wanted to understand the good and bad so I ended up with a journaling system that collects data composed of over two hundred indicators related to changes in income, savings, education, health, and housing — making sure I captured the positive actions they take. The journaling also tracks whether those enrolled in FII help some-one else or are helped because the extent of their friendships and connec-tions, their "social capital", heavily influences their lives. A partial list is in the chart below.

Income	Balance Sheet	Activities	Community
• Income from Employment	• Savings Account	*Education & Skills*	*Networking & Helping*
• Formal (W-2, 1099-INT)	• Checking Account	• Improved Grades	• Refers Friend to a Job
• Informal (Under the table)	• Cash On Hand	• Improved Attendance	• Helps Other Start Business
• Own Business	• Personal Loans Others Owe You	• After School Programs	• Refers Other to Resource
• Formal	• Credit Card Debt	• Graduation	• Helps Others in Crisis
• Informal	• Auto Loans	• Scholarships	• Expands Job Networks
• Type of Business	• Education Loans	• Adult Classes	• Recruits & Orients New FII Families
• Child Support	• Personal Loans Owed	• Workshops	
• Other Income (Not FII)	• Real Estate Loan	• Continuing Education	
• Supplemental Security Income	• Alimony		*Resourceful & Leading*
• Unemployment Income	• Child Support	*Health & Housing*	• Attent Trainings
• Lump Sums	• Other Debt/Obligations	• Insurance Coverage	• Shares Training
• Food Stamps	• Credit Score	• Preventative Care	• Involved/Lead Civic Activities
• Calworks/DTA		• Checkups	• Attends Leadership Workshops
• WIC		• Routine Test	• Leads FII Activities
• Subsidized Portion of Housing		• Immunizations	
• Other		• Therapy	
		• Mental Health	
		• Health Improvement	
		• Weight Loss	
		• Join Gym	
		• Blood Pressure	
		• Cholesterol	
		• Bought a Home	
		• Moved (Reasons)	
		• Improved Housing	

When families enroll with FII we have them enter baseline data related to the above indicators so that we can track subsequent changes. Each month they go online and update anything that changes. Since the families have to self-recruit a group of friends in order to join FII, we ask them to meet monthly so that our liaisons can hear the stories behind the data — what their goals are, how they are working to achieve them, and what challenges they face. Each quarter families allow us to verify what they enter through documents like pay stubs and report cards.

All of this takes up the family's time, therefore we pay families or give them access to scholarships, etc. for the time they spend giving us that information. Having the families enter the data and then only having to verify it is much cheaper than trying to have staff ask and enter the data, especially since we want data on a monthly basis. Families earn only a nominal amount for journaling and meeting, now on average around one hundred dollars a month. The cash itself is hardly life-changing given the hours they have spent to earn it, but we know that it does provide families a way to earn just a bit more each month, a small cushion.

The stories behind the data are critical to our understanding. When we noticed savings going down dramatically with one group, for instance, we learned anecdotally that group members were purchasing homes and the savings had been converted to equity in their new homes. One time there was a $5,000 jump in the savings of one of the families. The money turned out to be a reverse remittance from friends in El Salvador so that our enrolled family could buy a five-bedroom house in Pittsburg, California. The refugee families here were collaborating with friends back in their home country. They explained it was to be a "transition home for any other refugees coming from El Salvador". It was another example of low-income people taking care of their own in a way that a social service or housing program for refugees could never have designed. A contribution to society.

The information the families shared with us was helping us to better understand what families were doing for themselves and how they influenced one another. The results, as shown in the previous chapter, were more impressive than I had anticipated. The outcomes continue to improve and sustain. Our funders and stakeholders could barely believe the results we showed them. Even today policy makers and others that see how well the families do speculate that we are "creaming", that we have found a magic way to screen for families that would have succeeded anyway. I wish I was that smart. But it also indicates the presumption that low-income families aren't capable of significant change on their own.

When I was running the youth gang training program at AND, we used to bet on which of the kids coming in would succeed. None of us ever got it right. We might as well have flipped a coin. The ongoing success we have seen in FII families speaks to the invisible capability of families. But that capability begins to show when the professionals step back and instead just create an encouraging and trusting environment that offers choices.

Families see their own progress

Information is power. From the beginning the data collection system was designed so that FII families could see their own progress. As they enter changes in income, for instance, they can see a chart that shows the income line move up or down given what they entered over time. It is instant feedback. FII's journaling system is cloud-based and real-time so that the families can see the change as soon as they update the change. It is similar to apps such as Fitbit and Mint.com where you can see your physical or financial progress almost immediately. Families feel that access to this information is so beneficial that one of the families that dropped out of FII soon re-enrolled primarily for the feedback loop that let them take more control over their goals. "I used to keep up with my goals better when I was in FII and I saw what I had done or wanted to do each month," they explained. Another family reported that the entire family sits around the kitchen table each month to enter the data and see their progress. It has brought them closer together. Since families want to see their actual accomplishments, they are motivated to ensure that all of their data is accurate. Faking it doesn't do them or us any good.

The Ashers were typical of the first families we enrolled. They were a household of five and they showed an income of $1,400 a month ($16,800 annually) when they enrolled in FII. Peter was twenty-seven and worked in a landscaping business. Melinda was thirty-two, with no formal job but an ambition to start a housekeeping business. They were raising three children: one boy of nine, a boy who was four and a daughter three years old. They lived in East Oakland, a low-income district. Since their annual income meant that they fell below the poverty line — about $28,000 for a family of 5 — they were eligible for government support but they, like their friends, rejected it feeling it was demeaning.

Yet what didn't make sense to me as I looked at their finances was their rent — with utilities it came to at least $900 per month or more than half of their income. Other expenses for food, clothes, transportation and healthcare typically ran at least $1,000 a month, so this family's total expenses were likely $1,900 a month or $500 more than they reported that they earned. As FII gained their trust they shared that Melinda was cleaning the homes of some wealthy people and they paid her in cash which they initially hesitated to report. With her earnings and the recommendations from these wealthy families she was saving for a car and a good vacuum cleaner to expand her business. However, her expanding business meant she was not home to take care of the kids. The Ashers looked into childcare and afterschool care but the cost would have been more than Melinda could earn. It was the same circumstance my sister faced when she ran away from Chuck after a beating. This family didn't have a credit card or credit rating so they couldn't get a loan for the car. Peter and Melinda struggled over whether it would be best for her not to work and stay home. In the end, they found a grandmother of a friend to take care of their kids in return for Peter's care of her yard and some home maintenance.

There is a dollar value to this exchange and FII asks families to estimate the value of the exchange. The Ashers, like about a third of the families enrolled in FII, survive because of side cash businesses and the bartering or exchange of services. Peter and Melinda, like my mother and sister, were part of the U.S.'s hidden informal cash and barter economy. They were far from lazy. In fact they were doing exactly what Americans did historically to build our middle class. But since working in the informal economy is technically illegal, they hesitated to show us that ingenuity. Over time they did report all of their income and it continued to increase. We knew it was likely Melinda expanding her business.

For those interested in understanding the lives of those they seek to help it is important to build enough trust with families so they will share their resourcefulness. Rather than charity cases, the FII staff has come to admire the families we partner with.

Evaluations told us what really led to progress

While it helped families to see their own data and get paid for their time, what outside evaluators have determined is the greatest driving force for change is seeing what other similar families are doing. FII's online system includes dashboards that compare what each family is doing to what others are doing. Participants see only the combined change of others by group or city. Humans are competitive in nature. We are not just motivated by fear of missing out, but people seem to want to do better than their peers. Utility companies have learned that if they tell you on your bill that your neighbors are saving more energy than you, people strive to save more energy. "Social signaling" by peers is one of the most significant factors pushing and inspiring families to succeed. Traditional social programs will claim that the prime motivator in their clients' success is the training or counseling they receive from their program. I used to claim that when I ran social service programs. But what FII has learned is that sharing the personal successes of low-income families, like Javier and Maria buying a house, makes the biggest difference. The challenge for FII then became how to facilitate the sharing of the personal successes, the positive deviant and early adopter actions, beyond the initial cohort of friends.

UpTogether — Escaping poverty is a group effort

From 2001 to 2007 FII only had the journaling system for families. But once the families saw what others were doing, they wanted to connect directly with them and learn from one another. In 2006 FII enrolled families in Boston and San Francisco. As noted earlier, when some of the Boston FII families heard that families in San Francisco were forming lending circles, they wanted to do the same. They asked FII staff to connect them to the San Francisco families. But an underlying principle is for staff to never become central to their initiative.

At first we suggested that they use existing platforms such as Facebook or LinkedIn to connect directly with other families but they told us that they didn't trust what those services might do with the information they shared. The families were beginning to see each other as peers, even across the country.

Their feedback led to the creation of an FII-specific social networking site, resembling Facebook and LinkedIn, where our enrollees across the nation could connect with each other, form groups, make recommendations to one another or just chat. It took a few years to develop the site appropriately named *UpTogether*. FII families then began to connect locally and across the country. The personal monthly journaling system was a way for families to shape their lives, to be in *control* of their life. But UpTogether was about building a broader *community*; sharing, supporting and learning from others. They use the site to develop the strong and weak ties discussed earlier.

Growing up I remember that at the dinner table I often heard my mother or sister talk about what friends had accomplished or problems that they had overcome. Getting together with friends at the beauty salon, park or laundromat was where this information was often shared. The families we knew faced all the same problems we faced and some had found ways to overcome them or even what not to do. Those who discovered successful strategies were the positive deviants. At times we were the positive deviants, such as my mother's experience working at a car dealership made her the one others asked about how to get a good deal on a used car. The more people we knew the more positive deviant solutions we would find. There was no single leader, teacher, or program, but instead there was a myriad of *home-grown experts* that lived under similar circumstances.

UpTogether is set up to be the online beauty salon where sharing happens. It is where you can post your success or a new benefit, even a program that you want to recommend. FII is not against families referring each other to social service programs since it is their life. Our staff, however, lives in a different reality and their position gives them more power, so staff is not allowed to recommend. This is all about changing who the experts really are.

UpTogether is where families can crowd source solutions, as happens so often online today. The solutions developed by peers are more tangible and often much more useful than attending a training session. If someone learns something useful through experience or in a program they are encouraged to share it, to be the expert. Families love sharing their experiences with others. Social networking and technology reduces the need for paid professional staff to do these tasks, keeping costs down.

Every family in FII sets up a profile on UpTogether. Like Facebook there is a feed where participants can share accomplishments or ask for advice. Families also form groups so that they can work together. At times the interaction is only online and other groups meet face to face. There is a recipe group to share healthy food recipes; another group focused on social issues, yet another on computer skills.

Another basic premise of the *alternative* is that families are given choices or the flexibility to use financial awards as they decide. To test this FII has set up what it calls the *Resource Hub* that provides a variety of financial awards. The participating families play a central role in designing the eligibility criteria. The choice of resources includes matching funds for dollars they have saved to start a business or pay tuition for school, etc. There is also a low interest loan fund to test new underwriting criteria as well as matching dollars to other initiatives families take such as to improve their health. Below are two other resources available to FII participants.

FII Family Time Fund

Families, like mine, where the parents or guardians work long hours or multiple jobs often lack quality time to spend with their children. I remember asking my mother if she could take us to Disneyland. It took her two years to save enough money and get the vacation time needed, but when we finally went it was a huge bonding experience. The Family Time Fund makes events like this possible for FII participants by matching the savings of families so they can spend quality time together. Quality time with your children is priceless. And helping this happen costs only a few hundred dollars per family. Far less than my youth programs spent to have professional staff lead youth trips and events.

Berta Miller Scholarship Fund

Most families want their children to go to college but don't have the funds to make this dream a reality. When I got accepted to U.C. Berkeley there was no tuition, but now a college education in the United States can break a family's bank. Families tried to access scholarships but found it extremely difficult to identify and then meet the diverse criteria for each fund. FII started a scholarship fund named after my mother, the Berta

Miller Scholarship fund, with eligibility criteria that the families themselves helped develop.

UpTogether's Resource Hub also gives families online access to crowd sourced funds such as Kiva, Kickstarter, Benevolent, etc. As the variety of available resources grows, we track their use and the impact they have on the families.

One illustration of the Resource Hub's success is that of Bryan Wilson, a truck driver:

In 2010, Bryan saw the writing on the wall. The trucking company he was working for was starting to lay off workers. Instead of waiting for a pink slip, Bryan and his wife, Luz, decided to use their savings and start their own trucking company. To purchase a truck Bryan applied for a bank loan but was offered an interest rate of 23.5 percent because of their low credit score. Instead Bryan and Luz applied for, and received, a low interest loan through FII's Resource Hub. In addition they accessed FII's savings match, which matched their saving two-to-one. Bryan and Luz put a down payment on a truck and launched their business.

Since then Bryan has paid FII back and generated enough income to pay for the truck in full. Now he is partnering with a friend to expand his business and create more jobs. A $5,000 investment from FII yielded a $40,000 annual income increase for Bryan and Luz, who have now set their sights on buying a home for their family.

FII felt comfortable with making the loan and offering matching funds because the Wilson family had provided us verified data for over six months on all that they were doing to improve their lives. Friends also vouched for them. Families as resourceful and motivated as the Wilsons are good credit risks even if they didn't have a good or any formal credit rating. Just as the Irish in historic Boston would lend to each other based on reputation, FII is doing the same. Others can do the same. There are literally tens of thousands of families like the Wilsons that can show they are good credit risks and deserve backing.

These stories repeat and through UpTogether we can track the contributions they are making to society.

An Alternative Credit Score

FII is taking all the data it collects and is developing an alternative score that we, and others, can use to identify reliable and resourceful families. It is called the *Initiative Score*. The score is developed from a variety of qualitative and quantitative factors such as consistent participation in lending circles, volunteerism, income, net worth, and their reputation in their community like in the old days. Working with funders, banks and businesses, FII is now able to assist in providing enrolled families with choices of financial resources. In turn, private businesses can tap into a new set of reliable customers.

The San Francisco Foundation was the first to set funds aside that can go directly to families based on their Initiative Score. It is called the Direct to Families Fund or DFF. Families enrolled in FII for at least six months, with verified data, earn an Initiative Score. A score of over 600, for instance, can prequalify them for access to funds from the San Francisco Foundation's Direct to Families Fund. If they, for instance, have a sixteen-year-old that they are pushing to go to college, building their score will mean that when they get admitted to college a scholarship will be made available. The funds from the foundation's DFF fund will get transferred to FII, which will pass it on electronically to the family that applied. It is like pre-qualifying for a mortgage.

Similar DFF funds can be set up all over the nation or the world. As long as a family provides enough information about what they are doing to improve their own lives and help others, they are considered prequalified and can apply for anything from an award or fellowship to a low interest loan. Since they can generally only apply for one resource at a time, the families must set their own priorities and FII can thus see the demand whether it is family time or education. The data helps the family qualify, but it also allows FII and the funder to track their progress and the outcome of the awards that the family earns. Donors to the DFF fund at the San Francisco Foundation see quarterly reports about the progress the families make and that their investments make a difference that may create a ripple effect.

Imagine a business, such as Ford Motors, who wants to increase its sales. They may not know to which families they can prudently provide a lease or a car loan. If the Initiative Score can be added to their underwriting criteria, then suddenly they have grown their customer base. Like the Wilson family, a new trucking company emerges, taxes are paid, new jobs are created and everyone benefits.

The families are motivated to provide verifiable data, for example, so their next teen can also get a scholarship or they can expand their business idea. There are now waiting lists in all the cities that have FII enrolled families because this *alternative* approach attracts even more people to join and provide verifiable data. *Now instead of a race to the bottom, we have a race to the top!*

*

Unusual lessons learned

Gathering a broad range of data has also provided some unexpected lessons about the choices people make. People's lives are complex and the issues they face, from housing to their children's grades, are interconnected. Solving a problem is not necessarily a linear process as the data from families has shown FII. Outsiders rarely have a clear view of that interdependence.

Expanding business income:

Depending on locality, about 20 percent to 30 percent of families enrolled in FII have business income — from full-blown businesses to side businesses in the informal economy. In monitoring the choice of resources that families who are growing their businesses have sought, the largest number of requests were for investments that helped stabilize their families, rather than investments into the business itself. The requests are for matching funds for spending quality time as a family and with friends (family events), funds to help their children with school, fix leaks in their apartment or even transportation for their family. Ultimately it makes sense because you can't concentrate on growing your business if your family faces other priorities or needs.

Most nonprofit business expansion programs to help these families focus almost exclusively on funds to operate the business, ignoring family stability needs. Those who live a more privileged life take many of these stability issues for granted and ignore them in designing programs. As FII captures monthly data it is able to see that providing a wide range of choices for business owners is essential. Providing support in "silos" or restricted categories, slows progress. Having flexibility and choices is the key.

Another thing I have observed is that when one of my more privileged friends starts a business, there were a number of investment options available to them, whether from family, friends or angel investors. Their business first acquires "equity investments", not loans. Only after that equity amount is determined do loans come into play. The intent is to not strain the entrepreneur or business during what could be several years of losses until the business became profitable.

But for low-income families the first capital investment offered is debt. Micro-business programs targeting low-income families generally start by offering micro-loans, not equity investments. These already strained entrepreneurs have the added stress of making loan payments before their business can get off the ground. They don't have the rich uncle or angel investor to provide a startup or expansion cushion. Also, privileged entrepreneurs are expected to fail in their first ventures. Some Angel investors will only invest in entrepreneurs who have previously failed — and thus learned from those failures. Still low-income families continue to strive and should be admired, rather than blamed, if their businesses cannot grow at the same pace as the businesses of the more privileged. *Why are there two different systems of investment for entrepreneurs based on economic status?*

Improving children's educational attainment

Dorothy's three children were getting D's and F's in school when suddenly they began earning A's. At first we thought she had found an amazing tutoring program or intervention. What we learned is that the problem was solved when she purchased a used car so that she could get her children to school on time.

One of her children, Peter, has chronic asthma and must frequently stay home from school. On those days, she had to keep all of the kids home since she couldn't take her sick child on the multiple bus rides needed to reach the school. Now, with the car, she can take Peter with her when she drops her other children at school.

Most initiatives to improve educational attainment focus on creating programs at the school. Rarely do they try to understand the conditions at home. One national program, Health Leads, that works within hospitals, does a more comprehensive assessment of a family's needs and uses the status of the doctor to recommend support to pay a utility bill or even purchase a car.

Families need to drive the change

The story about Myong in chapter seven referenced that she had counselors from three different agencies to help her. One from my agency focused on her teenagers, another from the welfare department and yet another from the local refugee assistance program. But her life was not as complex as that of a family that had six counselors advising them! A reporter learned about all this help and asked the family how helpful all of that advise was. The client answered, "It would be more helpful if they could just help me pay my electricity bills."

What FII has learned is that social sector programs waste time and resources providing assistance that doesn't meet the real priorities of the families. Our experts and service providers have a very shallow, often siloed, view of the complexity of life in and around the poverty level. If the various programs want to be helpful, as well as protect their funding, they need to be more effective and efficient. They need to understand the issues from the perspective of those they want to help and not just the silo of help they represent. To truly assist in solving any problem they need to take direction from the very families they seek to help since *they are the experts of their own lives.*

CHAPTER TWELVE

Making the Invisible, Visible
Contributions by the bottom 2/5ths of our economy

In July of 2015, I attended a conference where Julián Castro, then Secretary of the U.S. Department of Housing and Urban Development (HUD), cited a 2015 report revealing that there was currently *no place* in the entire United States where a family living on minimum wage could afford a two-bedroom apartment, and only a couple places where they could afford a one-bedroom unit. Those working in the social sector on issues of housing or the minimum wage could use this study to lobby for more program funding. However, though well-intended, this perspective would again hide the resourcefulness of families. Secretary Castro did not address the reality that most of the families he was referring to, do live in one and two-bedroom units. How are they doing it? In the same way that my family and most low-income families do it; by working more than one job and maintaining side businesses in the informal cash economy.

CHAPTER TWELVE: MAKING THE INVISIBLE, VISIBLE

At the same event where Secretary Castro presented I sat next to a senior staffer from the Urban Institute, a national policy think tank. I asked if they had done any studies on the informal "cash under the table" economy (not prostitution and drugs). She didn't remember any but after the meeting she sent me the one study she found titled "Informal and Nonstandard Employment in the U.S.", published in 2011[24]. The researchers state that while there are many studies of the informal economies in other countries, very few look at that sector of our economy in the United States. If these studies existed we would have a more complete picture of the talents, economic power, and contributions of our low-wage workers. Then we could develop policies to recognize and invest in this ignored part of our economy. For many of the families enrolled in FII their efforts in the informal economy can easily be a quarter or more of their earnings. For some, the cash economy is how they subsist at all.

The informal, sharing, and bartering economy is what usually closes the survival gap for those who cycle in and out of the officially designated poverty income level. Our society ignores it because it has been classified as illegal even if not involving crime, drugs, or prostitution. These hidden micro economies were crucial in building our middle class. The Black Townships and Chinatowns started informally. It is in the informal economy where families are most free to show their interests and talents. Getting a job as a janitor or maid happens out of necessity. But independently doing construction, sewing, and selling tamales out of your kitchen, is a better indicator of talents, interests, and work ethic. These efforts also

---

24   This study pointed out some of the benefits of this part of our economy as well as policy changes that could recognize this sector. While most teenagers get their first jobs, like baby-sitting, in the informal economy, this economic activity is "concentrated among the poor". See Notes at the end of the book for the link to this and other studies cited.

contribute to our economy. We need to include these efforts as part of our economic assets, just as we have accepted the ways that the rich make money through financial instruments such as derivatives or the shorting of stocks.

Creating their own economy:

My mother and almost every family we knew did "side work", even if just before the Christmas holiday season. My mother worked two jobs and did sewing on the side. At heart she was a dress designer and an amazing seamstress. This side job is what really showed her talents. After we finished dinner and the ironing was done, I would often see her on her knees in the kitchen, newspapers spread flat on the floor. With my crayons, she would outline dress patterns. She could, somehow, adjust the pattern to any dress size.

"I saw a dress like this in a window" she would say, "and I could sell it for a quarter of what they are asking and still make money." She was exasperated because we didn't have the money she needed to start the business she wanted and still save for my college. There, on her knees, was when she seemed happiest, immersed in her talent. That's also when I felt happiest and content.

What no one recognized is that when she was happiest is when I did the best in school. This holds true in most any family. Relieving the stress in families, in parents, at home, has a more positive impact on children and teens than any youth program we design. At FII we have seen a correlation in the data showing that when families are gaining more control over their future, and are less financially stressed, their children's school attendance and grades improve. FII has not found that this improvement

166

correlates to any school program but it makes sense that everyone performs better when they are happiest.

Just as Daniel Beaty wanted his mother to dance, I wanted my mother to sew and start her own business. If it had become the dress or design shop she envisioned she would have also created jobs for others in our neighborhood. Most of our friends had some sort of side business, from teaching dance, to catering, or to landscaping. These businesses didn't just create jobs for the entrepreneur, but also for others. These jobs were, and still are, not counted in the national job creation statistics. Some become full time businesses and some never leave the home kitchen, but they all create jobs and provide needed services. Just as the Cambodian-run donut shops hired their teens so they could pay for college, these low-income entrepreneurs are engines of economic activity.

During the recession in 2009, the data FII was collecting on families showed that while they were losing jobs in the official economy their income wasn't going down in parallel. What we found is that people just became more entrepreneurial; cooking tamales, selling at the flea markets or cleaning homes. In Detroit, where the economy has been depressed for years, almost 30 percent of the FII families have substantial income from self-employment and small business activity.

Some of these businesses are licensed and some exist informally in the cash economy. Many wealthy families pay their maids and gardeners in cash so as not to have obligations as employers. Many businesses do the same. In many countries, especially third world countries, the informal economy can make up over eighty percent of the economic activity — hugely important. In the United States, the world's largest economy, the informal economy is estimated to make up between 10 percent and 20 percent of our economic activity. That is a lot of jobs, a lot of salaries, a lot of products being sold and a lot of taxes paid when products are bought.

The research organization, *Social Compact*, did a study referred to as the *Drill Down Study*, of the economy in Oakland, California, in 2004 when that city's population was 350,000. It found that like many cities with low-income populations, Oakland's informal economy (excluding drugs, prostitution, etc.), totaled $400 million annually. A similar study by Social Compact estimated that in Detroit, the informal economy in 2010 was $650 million. Most of that economic activity is centered in the lowest income neighborhoods. Unfortunately, however, since most of that initiative is hidden, there are very few ways to invest and grow it. As families in FII have sought support and investment, FII is testing different funds that can invest in the businesses, formal or informal. Banks and other funders can and should do the same.

Over the last 15 years of tracking families, the Family Independence Initiative studied some samples of this entrepreneurial activity and found that the family run businesses created on average 1.5 jobs each. The average investment to create each business was $2,000, much less than the $15,000 I spent in my previous service agency, AND, just to train and find a job for one young person like Richard.

One of the difficulties is getting all of these businesses and job creators recognized so that we can grow the jobs they create. Funders, whether government or philanthropic, too often only want to fund the big projects or the big corporations. In the West Oakland neighborhood mentioned earlier, public and private dollars in the millions have been used at least three times over two decades to develop a large grocery store in the neighborhood. The last publicly supported store was called Gateway Grocery. They all failed.

At the same time the West Oakland families were trying to start their own mom and pop grocery that would have featured healthy organic food, some grown by the families themselves. Their small corner store was on the tour that I gave to the board members of the California Endowment foundation referred to earlier. But neither the foundation or government would invest in that grocery store; or in the café, or art gallery or the community center, The Black New World, created by those families. Those from outside the community want a big store, a big project. Yet with much smaller investments, the combination of all of these smaller businesses could have created as many, if not more jobs for residents than Gateway Grocery. The families would have used or shopped at these various venues because they created them. They could have created their version of a Chinatown. There is a failure of seeing that starting small, looking at the steps people themselves are taking, and investing in them, is often better than the big, expensive ideas brought in from the outside.

Paying Taxes

During the 2012 presidential campaign, presidential candidate Mitt Romney was captured on a hidden video telling potential donors to his campaign that those in the bottom half of our economy do not pay taxes. Those listening likely believed him, as does a large portion of our country's population. While many lower income families don't pay much in federal income taxes, they do pay most other taxes, from property tax to sales and excise tax.

All of the families I grew up with, even if paid "under-the-table" for work, went out to buy food, shoes, and gas, feeding sales tax dollars into the economy. They rarely went to Italy or France to spend their money. When you calculate the percentage of income paid by low-income Americans in taxes, it turns out to be higher than that the percentage paid by the top one-fifth of our top earners in almost every State. The table below has the percent of income paid in Michigan. (See Notes)

Percent of State and local taxes paid in Michigan

	$15,000 or less	$15,001 to $32,000	$32,001 to $54,000	$54,001 to $86,000	$86,001 or more
Sales Tax	7.2%	5.7%	4.4%	3.5%	1.8%
Property Tax	2.0%	2.5%	2.7%	3.0%	2.7%
Income Tax	-0.3%	1.7%	2.7%	3.1%	3.3%
Total Tax Paid	8.9%	9.9%	9.5%	9.1%	6.8%

In most States the taxes paid by low-income families represent a full third of the tax base for the cities and states. State and local budgets couldn't survive without these tax revenues.

It is the accumulation of tens of millions of local transactions that naturally create value to society. I lived in Oakland when that city's Chinatown district was first forming and much of the economic activity was informal. Now Oakland's Chinatown rivals the well-known San Francisco Chinatown. The taxes that Oakland's Chinatown produces for the city of Oakland are an important part of the city's tax base.

Informal efforts have always been a key to building our economy and rather than classifying them as illegal we should recognize that initiative and find ways to invest in those efforts. Tax credits for self-employment and for angel investors to these businesses are but a couple ways to grow these micro-economies.

Undermining or ignoring contributions

Too often, in our quest to be charitable, to gain attention to inequality and social justice, we ignore or hide what families can do for themselves and the positive things they do for others.

In 2013, I visited a beautiful affordable housing development in Southern California which housed 230 low-income families. The units are subsidized and families pay only one-third of their income for rent. It has a pool and it is well-maintained. Children were running around happily. It appeared idyllic. I was there to meet with some of the residents, many of whom had been living in the development for more than a decade. The developer wanted to encourage them to move on to economic independence so that their apartments would be available for other families in need. I agreed to try to find out what would incentivize them to move out.

Over fifteen families showed up to meet with my staff and me in the community room. We asked the families if they envisioned leaving such an idyllic housing situation and, if they did, what was holding them back. To my surprise, most of the families wanted to leave — to own a home or to live in a different part of town — but feared it was financially impossible. They spoke about how subsidized housing regulations discouraged them from saving money or working more. Since their housing was designed for low-income occupants, they had to stay low-income. If their income or savings went up, their rent would go up as well, offsetting some of their income gains. Welfare works the same way. The families were all grateful to live in such an exceptionally beautiful housing project, but felt the system that supported it also acted as a trap. They didn't know of an alternative way to bridge the loss in rental subsidy and let them transition to the private housing market. Many seemed resigned to the situation.

"It is great that our kids feel safe and we have this community center," said one person. "Donna (the manager of the project) is really helpful. We can go to her with our problems and she organizes activities for us."

Then a couple in their thirties who had lived there for more than ten years recalled the period before the community center was built and Donna had been hired to run it.

"Remember when we used to do the *Week Without Kids?*" she exclaimed with excitement.

"Yeah, some of us would take the kids on a trip and it was so nice to have some free time here without them!" exclaimed another. Other families confirmed this, excitedly.

"And the *Kids Olympics* we had," said another family member.

"Oh, the picnics, too," and, "The camping trips," someone else chimed in.

And so the conversation became a boisterous back-and-forth among the long-time residents of the project, about all that they had voluntarily done before Donna was hired.

Eventually I asked the group, "So, why aren't you doing those activities anymore?" There was an awkward pause. A few of the residents looked at one another hoping to hear an answer.

"Well, Donna does a good job with activities," the couple who started this conversation answered, as the excitement in the room died out. I looked at my colleagues who were also realizing that by building the community center and staffing it, the housing project had ended the families' self-organizing and the pride that came with it. I am not against building community centers or hiring wonderful people like Donna, but public assistance should first and foremost support people to build a sense of community themselves. Before trying to help we must first find what people are already doing for themselves and keep those efforts central. The financial structure of affordable housing units also needs to be restructured so that it is transitional housing, except for the seniors and disabled that need it on the long term. *So much of what we believe and do around issues of poverty is wrong.*

As FII has tracked some of the other contributions enrolled families make to society we find they grow food and share it with needy neighbors, they clean up where their kids walk to school, and they take seniors and disabled to programs or doctors. A nonprofit service provider may see similar needs and then go to funders to start a food, clean up or transportation program. To get funded they have to convince funders that they are the *only* ones that can or will provide that service. They thus hide local initiative. Funders can change this. Their requests for proposals should ask those seeking funds to first discover what people are doing for themselves and others, and then explain how their services will enhance, rather than hide, those efforts. Then those efforts could grow and sustain even if the nonprofit drops the project.

This is not a call for outside volunteers or "points of light" as President Bush advocated. We need to support the residents themselves and their voluntary actions. This will also help to change the stereotype that they are helpless unless a program comes to save them. Institutionalizing solutions hides or discourages self-help, self-determination, mutuality and volunteerism. Recognition and encouragement increases self-help efforts.

Making us safer

My view of safety in our tougher neighborhoods comes both from my experiences growing up in those neighborhoods as well as working in them. Watching TV shows and movies it seems that violence is controlled because of some tough hero like those played by Clint Eastwood as the roguish cop in *Dirty Harry* or the caring neighbor in *Grand Torino*. But that is not what I observed or lived with.

In 2007, Donnell, the twenty-five-year old son of Sylvia, an FII enrolled family, was killed in a drive by shooting in North Oakland. He had left the gangs and it may have been someone else in the van who was the target. Donnell was working and building a good life for himself. Both of his parents were very proud of him.

I attended the funeral held at a corner church in the middle of the neighborhood. As I drove up I saw several young men standing watch at each of the corners about a block from the church in every direction. I also noticed one police car parked a little over a block away. Several young men stood watch by the overflowing church. I was able to only get into the doorway from where I could see the mass of people sitting, with Donnell's closed casket in front.

After a number of friends spoke about Donnell's life and how he had gotten his life together, his mother took the podium. Losing a child has to be the most inexplicably tragic moment in any parent's life, but there she stood, holding back tears, as she recounted details of her son's short life. She expressed her pride in how he was brave enough to leave the gang. Even with opportunities so limited for young black men he faced those challenges and made great strides. Her story was not intended to inspire pity. It inspired admiration.

But then she paused, leaned forward over the podium, and took a slow look at all those attending. Besides parents and friends, dozens of young men and women who knew Donnell stood and sat listening, and so she turned to them.

"Let me tell one thing" she said, as her finger pointed and moved across the room. "We are so tired of losing you. Of losing our sons and daughters. What I know is that Donnell would not want you to retaliate. Do you hear me? You can't retaliate! This has to stop. It has to stop here with my son!" Her voice rose. Pointing to his coffin in front of her she continued "This is his sacrifice and you have to honor him. He would not want you to retaliate, he wouldn't." She went on for some time lecturing and imploring all the young people attending to absorb the tragedy of all this. She then spoke to everyone, "It is all of our responsibilities to stop this, just stop this!" And the other parents chimed in agreement.

I monitored the news for stories of retaliation but I don't think it happened. Sylvia had stopped it and probably not just by that speech but because she pushed everyone, young and old, to take responsibility to stop the violence.

The police gang task force could have tried adding more patrols and could have stopped and frisked every young black man in the neighborhood but it would just have added to the tension. The city could have started new youth programs or the Mayor could have made an impassioned speech asking for the violence to stop. But I'm sure Sylvia's words and the actions of all those attending is what made it safer for everyone.

Some believe that these shootings go on because the adults in the neighborhood don't do anything to stop it. But it could be, and likely is, just the opposite. In my work, and from growing up in these neighborhoods, I know the families and adults are the ones who have kept these neighborhoods from exploding because of pent up anger. We must all consider what point of view to accept. Should we invest in a police "stop and frisk" approach or should we invest in the very people that our society distrusts but that do so much even facing personal losses. Like Sylvia and her neighbors, the Iu Mien parents continue their unrecognized vigilance. *Our ordinary heroes, parents and adults, should be honored and respected.*

CHAPTER THIRTEEN

THE *ALTERNATIVE*
Resurrecting the American Dream

The *alternative* is fairly simple; look for what people are already doing for themselves and others, and then invest in it. Follow, rather than
lead "them". This encourages and creates even more initiative. This ad-
dresses most of the flaws pointed out in the first section of the book. The
most basic impact is that trusting the families to lead their own change is
respectful and encourages even more progress, ultimately changing entire communities. FII has demonstrated that our society should trust the
families as experts of their own lives. It has shown that people are more
than willing to help one another and will follow the best examples set by
families like their own. Lastly, FII is demonstrating that if we provide
benefits, as we provide benefits to the rich, based on their initiative, then
you expand our economy and challenge many of the prejudices our society
has about "them".

To make this approach into a system that works at scale and helps a population, a region, a country or the world, it requires three steps:

1.   The first step is to collect direct information from a sample of the targeted population about what they are doing to improve their lives, *as well as* to help others. FII has already demonstrated how to do this using technology but it can also be done through surveys and other direct outreach. Do not rely on the usual experts, focus groups, perceived representatives or research studies. Go directly to the families without pre-assumptions or your own bias. The California Endowment and the Knight Foundation both hired polling companies to directly survey families about issues these foundations cared about, which proved effective in getting real information, at least on those issues. To establish strategies for socio-economic mobility and long term change I have found that going directly to families repeatedly, over time, provides information that that you will never get from the poverty "experts" or social service programs. Just as Walmart and Amazon look at purchase data *continuously*, if we want to make our helping system useful, we have to get ongoing information directly from the target families. They are willing to share it if they benefit in return. Ongoing data collection is important because the benefits or connections my mother searched for when I was four years old were entirely different when I was five and in school. Also, what would have helped my sister or mother changed, often in short intervals. You never know when a new job may be available or when your car will break down.

       It is also important that the collected information is shared with the families themselves. Families should see their personal data as well as the cumulative data about peers that is collected by funders and service providers. Having the data available to the families is not only a huge driver of change but it adds to the transparence of the project. It develops trust between the families and those that want to be helpful. In our current helping system families rarely see the data, stories, or strategies that the service providers or experts share with each other. Transparency is important.

Lastly, rather than having professional programs or counselors as the center of information, funders and programs need to encourage and facilitate ways for the families to network and share information with one another directly, much as Save the Children did in Vietnam. The information a family gains from someone who has already experienced a similar situation is much more useful than the information from a counselor not living in the same circumstance. FII offers to pay for the food or venue if families self-organize meetings or clubs. On UpTogether families can also meet virtually and they can share advice and crowd source solutions. Information is power.

2. The second step is to analyze the data and align resources so that they support the actions that families are already taking to get ahead. Just as Walmart and Amazon analyze the data they have on purchases to determine what products to sell to you, this *alternative* system can do a similar analysis to determine the benefits — scholarships, family time match, loans, etc. — that are most appropriate for various populations or at different locations. Data scientists have developed a myriad of tools — regression studies, geospatial mapping, text mining — to not only tell us what is happening in real time but to also predict what might happen in the future. These tools can be used in

the social sector. Small start-up businesses track this data and so even small nonprofits can do this if the funders will support those actions. FII is already using an algorithm that identifies families that are fully credit worthy even if they don't have a formal credit rating. Because of the data FII gets from families, we are able to watch the behavior patterns of mother's, like my mother, and know that they are trying to save for their child to go to college. A scholarship can then be set aside for that family if that pattern continues. If something like that had existed for my mother, she may not have gotten the bleeding ulcers that made her life miserable. Resources, such as those described in chapter eleven, can be formed to address local demand. Most families will give up some of their privacy if the benefits are tangible and accessible.

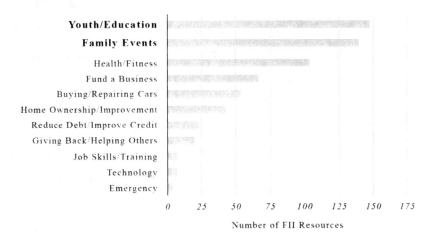

As FII tracked what families did with these small awards or matching dollars we saw that the families prioritized support for their children and strengthening the family unit. Above is a chart documenting the uses that the families prioritized in requesting support through FII's Resource Hub. It is clear that family and children are the priority for most everyone. *Most kids do not have the "wrong parents".*

The other interesting finding is that the cost per youth impacted was only a few hundred dollars, much less than what I would routinely spend in the more traditional youth programs I ran for twenty years.

3.   The last step needed to make the *alternative* approach effective, is to promote a sense of community, of mutuality. That requires getting professional helpers out of the way. What FII evaluators found was that the primary driver of success for FII families was the peer effect; positive deviance and diffusion of innovation theory. People need each other and thus they influence each other. Friendships and family cannot be replaced by professional staff, no matter how nice or well-meaning. Instead, programs and funders can financially support self-organized events or gatherings promoting friendship, and a sense of community. *Being friendless is the deepest form of poverty.*

My son's college, Drexel University, like other colleges, encouraged students to form clubs as a way of developing camaraderie and leadership skills. Any group of students that formed a club for most any purpose was allocated $400 by the University to do whatever activities the club planned, even if, as my son shared, it was going to football games for research. When FII offered similar funding to enrolled families, sure enough, they came together to do yoga, share recipes, or to distribute food to others in the community. At those club gatherings they shared ideas and provided support to each other, much as used to happen at the beauty or barber shop in the old days.

FII also built UpTogether, a virtual meeting and sharing place, where people can share and crowd source ideas.

There are those that believe that the sense of community is diminishing and that it can't be resurrected. But it is more likely that as a society we actively discourage people from getting together. We don't do enough to encourage the mutuality that happens when people come together. We should validate and facilitate low-income families as the best counselors for one another.

To test whether the sense of community and mutuality could be strengthened, FII asked families to recruit their friends in order to join. Also, FII had our staff step back so that families could step up with their own ideas and leaders. By firing staff that tried to help, we made it clear they had to look towards one another for support. When we began tracking people's efforts to help each other in this kind of empowering environment we found that, within six months, acts of mutuality jumped over 30 percent.

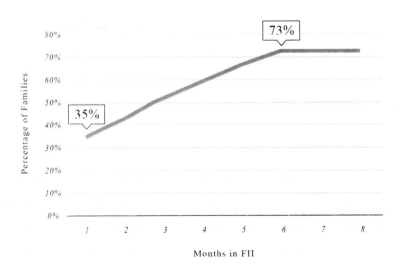

Much of what FII has learned, and I experienced growing up, leads to a simple *alternative*. We must trust families about their own lives. However, trusting the families runs counter to so many current practices and assumptions. It threatens current jobs, current services, current funding approaches, and current experts. But it is the common sense approach that ultimately serves everyone.

*

CHOICES

Make poverty tolerable or escapable?
Investing in initiative and talent is how to create upward mobility

For those concerned about the growing class and wealth gap, there is a choice to make. Some can choose to provide charity — professionally run services to relieve the pain of poverty — others can choose to invest in the initiative that families are already taking so they can build their own lives and truly escape poverty. The difference between efforts to make poverty tolerable or escapable is a distinction that the social sector tends to ignore. One requires charitable outsiders to lead the change. The other requires the families who wish to improve their lives to lead their own change. Our biggest accomplishment in the fifty-year-long war on poverty has been to make living in poverty tolerable for some. The social service sector has invested in providing subsidized housing, food and even child-care programs, and all that is important. These benefits remain available as long as you stay tolerably poor. However, my mother and our friends did not come to the United States to live in tolerable poverty. No one grows up wanting to be a welfare queen.

Some subsidized services, like childcare, can be vital for achieving upwardly mobility but currently access to services like these is not tied to upward mobility, as the story about Margaret and Ruben, her special needs child, illustrated in chapter two. If anything, you are more likely to qualify for assistance if you *don't* show evidence of upward mobility. If you show too much progress you will lose the benefit. It is also important to understand that charity can erode dignity and can undermine the authority of parents, even if it is welcome when in crisis. Charity cuts into the dignity of people because we are in a society that looks down on those that are poor. Low-income families are acutely aware that accepting government or even philanthropic help classifies them as "takers" from society. Low-income parents are not trusted and are viewed as incapable of making good decisions. Racism, sexism and other ism's all add to this psychological burden. The current distrustful environment and the extent of prejudice is just another barrier low-income families face. Therefore, until the contributions of those at the bottom of our economy are recognized and respected, accepting charity only adds to the negative stereotype.

Charity in itself is not a bad thing. When the homeowners after hurricane Sandy got charity — shelter and food — it was a very positive effort. The distinction being made is that because they were homeowners they were considered contributors to society. The perception of homeowners as contributors meant their social status, their self-confidence, their role as authority figures with their kids, was not diminished. But charity to those after Katrina, to a population viewed as primarily of color and poor, was slow in coming partly because of perceived negative stereotypes of the population there. The challenge is to shift the narrative so that low-income families are *also* recognized for their many contributions, rather than viewed as charity cases who can't take care of themselves.

We need an *alternative* system that highlights and invests in the millions of contributions, right steps and good decisions people make; Ben who was trying to leave the gangs, Mrs. Thompson who was advocating for her sons, the Iu Mien people and the Mardi Gras Indian tribes in New Orleans. When we succeed in breaking the negative stereotypes, then accepting charity during a crisis will no longer be a problem for the low-income.

For anyone who has raised teenagers, or has ever been a teenager (I think I got most of us), it is a pretty common sense insight that focusing on our children's talents and demonstrated initiative will be what provides the best chance for their future success. Libraries, health, education, and decent meals are important but in and of themselves are not life changing. In high school my son would stay up all night hacking web sites, learning all the graphic software he would use in college. His academics suffered but he was demonstrating his interests and talents. He is now doing amazingly well as a graphic artist. From the time she could hold a pencil my daughter would draw. I realize that I should have just supported that initiative, instead of trying to get her to do soccer or ballet. Both of my children have clearly defined their interests and talents and are doing wonderfully. As artists they have defined their own measures of success in a way that no one from the outside, even their parents, could have.

Funders and programs want clearly defined measures of success. Yet defining success is the business of the family and each member of that family. It is not the purview of politicians or social service programs. Low-income families and their children need to have the range of choices that my children had and, as previous chapters have pointed out, these are choices that our society can make available.

The Family Independence Initiative collects data monthly from our member families and from that data we see what those families are doing to improve their lives. Are they learning to cook healthy meals and enrolling in college and helping others? The families are willing to provide that information because FII's *alternative* approach can then provide a range of choices of resources or connections based on their initiative. Those of my colleagues who want to focus on upward mobility can do the same.

While some of us in the social sector need to continue to provide charitable assistance so that kids don't go hungry or sleep in the rain, others working with low-income families — funders, nonprofits and even businesses — need to recognize the initiative people take on their own. Then we need to designate at least half of the funds we spend making poverty tolerable and instead use those dollars to directly invest in the initiative and talents that families and their children take of their own volition. Those homegrown solutions are the ones that will scale and the cost is significantly less than professionally run programs.

Our country, and the world, needs to have the hard conversation that distinguishes between efforts that primarily help make poverty tolerable, and efforts that lead to sustained upward mobility. If we want to address income, wealth, and social stratification, we have to invest in what people are already doing to get above the poverty line and help them to work together and grow that initiative. Funders, policy makers, government bureaucrats, and conveners of conferences need to separate the discussions of programs aimed at making poverty tolerable from those aimed at sparking upward mobility. The tenor of the environments required for fruitful discussions are totally different.

In the charitable environment, the professional is the leader, sharing their ideas and expertise. Most current conferences convene these experts and encourage them to lead. These discussions call for more innovation or programs from the top, by those who control resources.

In the environment needed to discuss the *alternative,* the professional is more subservient, a "follower leader" is what my friend Kouichoy calls it. At least half of the participants should be from the targeted populations. Those that are professionals or paid staff of an organization need to hold back in these conferences, creating a vacuum of leadership, so the families can step up. We must change the current power dynamic of these discussions. The *alternative* environment has to carry the message that the families are the experts and will lead, and that those that want to help, the outsiders, will play a more supportive role. Like FII staffers Wandy and Paola explained in chapter ten, it sometimes takes a while to transition to being a "follower leader".

Large scale change? — ripple up
Policy and programs can diminish naturally occurring solutions and progress

The narrative that to get big change you need big programs or big policies is flawed. In a report, Daniel Zingale, senior vice president at the California Endowment, wrote:

"The phrase "culture eats strategy" is commonly used to make the point that inside workplaces and other organizations, even the greatest strategic plan will crash and burn if it clashes with the internal culture. But the phrase can also be applied to ways in which we try to make changes in our society. There are countless examples where our politics and policies changed only after prevailing norms shifted."

To bring about fundamental change we must focus on creating a cultural shift so that subsequent policies will be honored, not the other way around. You don't get rid of racism by passing legislation. Negative attitudes and actions towards one another have to be identified, challenged, and changed on the ground. Policy and legislation rarely does that and often obscures deep seated perspectives. The 2016 presidential election revealed that our country had not dealt with the cultural shifts needed if we are to unite. Policies and political correctness hid deeply embedded attitudes. Too often just the terminology changed, but attitudes didn't.

A friend, who lives in one of the more conservative neighborhoods over the hills from my hometown of Oakland, told me that years ago her neighbors would complain to the police when they felt "too many *blacks* were showing up" at a local club. She heard that the police would begin to harass the patrons or find reasons to threaten closing the club. As it became politically incorrect to specify "blacks" as the target, she heard an adjustment in the terminology. "Now my neighbors call the police and say the club has gone *Oakland*". My hometown of Oakland is identified as having a large black community. After the 2016 presidential campaign, even those barriers of incorrectness may be lifting.

Policies do not overcome imbedded cultural attitudes. We need to change the information and interactions people have with one another. Policies and programs too often placate or obscure rather than solve. Like so much of what is done by my colleagues in the social service sector, policies are not *bad* things to spend time and funding on, but they tend to distract us away from focusing on the importance of cultural shifts. They obscure the need for a fundamental change in personal attitudes.

Therefore, some work on policy should continue but it must be balanced by supporting work that encourages and lifts up the self-organizing efforts and traditions that bring about larger cultural shifts. The Iu Mien community initially waited for programs and policies to solve the problem of their youth going into gangs. But ultimately the families organized themselves to bring about that change. They focused on speaking personally with each teen, strengthening their sense of village, and strengthening the respect for their culture and religion. They personally went door to door and invited neighbors of every ethnicity to the community center they built in East Oakland. Policies and programs could not replicate the impact of one culture welcoming others. Working together, these families permanently changed the trajectory of their youth from prison to college. They created a tipping point within ten to fifteen years. And if their initiative had been quickly recognized and rewarded that change could have happened so much faster. *Lives were at stake.*

Large-scale cultural or behavioral shifts happen more like Malcolm Gladwell explained in his book *Tipping Point*. Shifts come from the internalized values and roles of the people themselves. To get positive change outsiders must first recognize the thousands of right things that people are doing for themselves. Those are the changes most likely to grow and sustain on the long term. The policy makers, nonprofits, and funders, must *learn how to learn from the families themselves.*

With so much that is positive already happening in our low-income communities we can suspend the social sectors fascination with outsiders as "social innovators" or new "theories of change." There will be room for new outside ideas and innovations once the innovations from the families themselves carry the same credibility and can also draw funding and recognition. Services will be needed and professionals can help, but they have to follow — not supplant — natural mutuality and personal initiative.

The example of how Javier and Maria's effort to purchase a home, the expansion of lending circles, are some of the many efforts already in place. Those that want longer term change can simply support those natural efforts. If, for instance, some of the funds we currently spend on programs instead went to match the funds that people are already pooling in lending circles we would not only double or triple the positive outcomes (businesses, college, etc.) happening, but the recognition of those self-financing efforts would encourage even more families to follow that example, maybe reaching a tipping point. Policy efforts can support the creation and expansion of informal lending circles, but efforts to make it into a program, to institutionalize it, will kill the sense of community and trust that helps rebuild relationships, rebuild mutuality. You would never want to institutionalize bar mitzvahs or quinceaneras. Relationships are sometimes messy, but as with informal lending circles they become self -regulating and sustaining as illustrated by the quotes below.[25]

> "We all work in the same hotel. Every week we save $30 and each of the twelve of us receive a payout of $360 four times a year. We are all from Mexico."

---

25   These quotes came from interviews collected by Jeffrey Ashe as part of the Carsey School of Public Policy, University of New Hampshire. Lending circles are just one of the strategies families use to survive and move ahead in low-income communities,

"If someone does not pay they will not only be blackballed from our group but every other savings circle in the Haitian community."

"I am in a group of twenty where we save $100 each, every week. I use my $2,000 payout to take care of my child who often gets sick with asthma."

"Black, Haitian, Latino, Chinese; we all do it. Why not learn from each other?

The importance of personal, voluntary efforts that benefit themselves and friends cannot continue to be ignored. The economic power of self-financing cannot be ignored and should be matched by outside sources. The best ideas do not necessarily come from the privileged, the paid professionals, or charismatic leaders. Institutionalizing or professionalizing what are personal efforts will actually kill them. Personal informal commitment is what was important and is what stopped the gang wars for the Iu Mien. Others can follow that example.

Having the option to get funding is not a bad thing if what it does is match rather than lead the change families are undertaking for themselves. This is an important distinction. If you try to lead with money or rewards as the driver of change, you can undermine or misdirect the commitment to voluntary action and sustained change. In communities that have been disempowered, we must wait for a homegrown idea to blossom and be owned by the person or community, before offering money. The small grocery store started by a group of residents in West Oakland showed they had skin in the game and were committed. That was the time to invest. We need these positive deviants and/or early adopters. This takes patience by funders and social activists who are used to being in front and leading the charge.

What FII has learned is that if funds are made available *after* voluntary efforts begin to take root, after the idea has been tested or is being tested by the early adopters, then the efforts towards self-determination will multiply. People appreciate that their efforts first are recognized and can eventually lead to rewards. We have also learned that the *biggest "reward" is the personal satisfaction families get by creating, being in control of the change, of directing their own progress, and making things better for themselves and others,* as so many research studies have found.

Many of those that have found FII "interesting" often believe that the access to dollars is what makes for FII's success. Funds are important to families living on the margins but without the respect for the "self-determination" that the West Oakland families spoke about or without people being "active in their own destiny", as Linda suggested, money alone will fail. Just offering money, as with passing policies or providing services, does not change the sense of control people need over their lives. That is why a program tried in New York city, the Conditional Cash Transfer, CCT, programs, did not lead to the sustained change it hoped for. It offered cash awards if participants took predefined actions set up by the program (get a library card, go for financial training, etc.). This is a bit like offering vouchers, which show a distrust of people to make their own decisions or set their own priorities. These programs do not signal that the families are trusted, in charge, and thus responsible for their own lives. The rich or poor want that responsibility, especially if they are given choices that let them take control.

It has to be emphasized that the success FII families have demonstrated is because of the trusting environment we have created. The participants have come to realize that they are in charge and we, the professionals, are the ones learning. If our country also trusted and respected families to lead their own change, then change could accelerate.

The reason the *alternative* can reach scale is because positive actions are constantly happening in every neighborhood and if our society recognizes these home-grown efforts and invests in these efforts, we can get *millions of tipping points, everywhere;* like those in the Iu Mien and in the Salvadoran communities. There is no silver bullet, no single tipping point. There wasn't just one path for May's family, or the Cambodian families, to follow.

The change in the stereotype of Asian youth, from gang members to college graduates that happened over the last fifty years is due to progress made following multiple paths forged *internally* in that community. That community faced discrimination but rather than counting on programs or policies, many Asian families focused on strengthening cultural ties and ethnic pride. Strong enclaves formed and, like May's family, many worked together in a variety of self-defined ways. There was a cultural and generational shift in expectations and actions that broke the 1960s stereotype of Asians as laundry workers or mysterious gangsters.

The fifty black townships in Oklahoma did not arise after slavery because of policies, programs, or the leadership of outsiders. The current stereotype could have changed if the efforts of those communities had not been burned down.

The social systems shift needed in this country is to accept that we must build from the efforts of the members of the community themselves. There are positive deviants and role models in every community if we seek to recognize them.

Humans are diverse and you will never "package" them: the Salvadoran refugees, the Iu Mien, the Mardi Gras tribes, the parents being organized by Margaret around their special needs children or the women in FII self-organizing to support each other around domestic violence. If a nonprofit or research study finds a real need or problem in a community, you can be certain that there are people facing that problem who are coming up with solutions that outsiders could support so they would spread. By getting ongoing data from the families FII can see these efforts expanding and some reaching tipping points. *Success is that people are gaining enough confidence to come together voluntarily around things that are important to them.*

For those wanting to be helpful, rather than looking for people's weaknesses, hold back judgement and hold back on the solutions we as outsiders come up with. Let people rise to whatever level they choose without pre-judgement. Create a vacuum of leadership so they can step up for themselves. Let their creativity and resourcefulness come out and be rewarded. Only then can we imagine the millions of solutions, the millions of tipping points, and the fundamental change in how we would view one another across class, race, religion or region.

Putting boxes, programs, frameworks, or institutions around people is the best way to kill or slow initiative and cultural shifts. Humans are wonderfully unique! As Daniel Pink pointed out, whether you are rich or poor, there is a *"deep human need to direct our own lives, to learn and create new things, and to do better by ourselves and our world."*

CHAPTER FOURTEEN

Epilogue
Would my mother approve?

I hope that my mother would approve of this new system, the *alternative*, that FII is demonstrating. It recognizes hard work, talents and provides mechanisms for investing in initiative. She only needed a better sewing machine, some fabric, and some funds to start her business and with that income she could have saved more for my schooling while not having to be away in the evenings. It would also have helped if, in recognition of how hard she and I were working to save, that scholarships would have been available. I wasn't a straight "A" student but our efforts should have qualified us. Most people are ordinary like us. Very little help is available unless you are super smart or in super trouble. If we want most people's lives to improve then we must invest in the ordinary folks like us. They don't need large investments.

My mother's challenge to me when I was ten was clearly not just about my life or my sister's life. She didn't want the difficulties faced by our family to happen to other families and their children. My mother had a deep sense of justice, of fairness. She wanted better for her children but also for all children. She couldn't accept losing a child, any child, to bad circumstances or death. I was reminded of her by an HBO movie, *The Girl in the Café*, that portrays my mother's deepest sentiments about our need to assure a good future for all children.

The movie quotes the sad fact that world wide a child dies needlessly, deaths we can prevent, every 3 seconds, 30,000 a day. The female protagonist snaps her fingers "there they go" and three seconds later she snaps them again "and another one!" Later in the movie there is a scene where Bill Nighy, who plays a negotiator of the G8 Millennium Development Goals, asks this girl who he met at a Café why she had been in prison. She replies, "I hurt a man." "Why?" he asks. "Because he had hurt a child. Killed a child." Bill follows up, "Your child?" to which she responds, "Does it matter whose child?" That's the point. It doesn't matter whose child.

The day that my mother left for her trip to Las Vegas where she took her life, she called me to say her last goodbye, though I didn't know it. She caught me at work first asking me how I was and if things were going well. Then she told me she was going to Las Vegas for the weekend. She had done that before. But then at the end she spoke softly, extending each word as if each word was a sigh. "Mauricio, sabes que te quiero mucho, mi hijo" or 'Mauricio, you know I love you very much, my son.'

I was at work and people were asking me questions and I was distracted but I did grasp that this goodbye was different than others. Still I just answered, "Yes and I love you too". As I look back I feel I should have known what was going to happen. I should have stopped to ask or talk or at least tell her with much more care how much I loved her too. But I just said goodbye. I'm still saying goodbye.

"Sometimes it falls upon a generation to be great.
You can be that great generation."

Nelson Mandela, 2005

Acknowledgements

This book has been in the making for many years, frustrating some friends .... "finish it already!" So finally, thank you for their patience.

My mother, Berta, is the first I need to acknowledge. It is her sense of social justice, in non-political terms, that shaped my values. It was her strength, determination, and resourcefulness that continues to drive me and her love that sustains me. She was not an easy person to be with and she was the only person whose judgement could really hurt me. But parents are often difficult, until you realize how readily they would give their lives for you. So, thank you again, Mom.

I also want to thank the families and communities of families who have shared their stories and inspired me. Only a few of their thousands of stories appear here.

Thanks also to my children who helped staff tables at FII family events and who stayed supportive as I left a perfectly good job to take on this journey to find an *alternative*. It has been amazing to get advice from them and to work with my son, Nick, who has done all the graphics and design for this book.

Next, there are so many that I have been privileged to work with as we together shaped this *alternative*. First is Jerry Brown whose challenge to think without restriction inspired FII as the demonstration of the *alternative*. The staff of the original FII-Oakland project; Marisa Castuera, Tracie Haynes, Molly Clark, Anne Stuhldreher and the wonderful Michelle Chao who remains working with me. Also, my thanks for the creativity and support of the current FII leadership provided by Jesus Gerena and Jorge Blandon who continue this quest to change the country.

I've had the support of so many others who have inspired me or have backed this counter-culture experiment: Bob Friedman and his beautiful mom, Phyllis, Tony Mayer, Chuck Parrish, and my good friend Sherry Hirota. Carrie Fox who volunteered to help with outreach. Michele Jolin who introduced this effort to the President and First Lady, Michelle Obama. Also, Patty Stonesifer who stopped the work of a commission set up by President Obama and asked, "Are we missing something? The role of the families themselves?" She helped in many other important ways.

Also, many thanks to those who helped edit the various versions of this book including John Raeside, Tamara Straus and Danielle Gerena, as well as friends who read and gave me feedback.

Lastly, I want to acknowledge that this book is often more critical of well-intended colleagues than it is of those whose prejudice would keep them from ever trusting families like mine. My belief is that my colleagues can come together and empower families like the one I was raised in.

Notes

Introduction

Deficit theory is closely related to the idea of the "culture of poverty," term first coined in 1961 by Oscar Lewis in his book *The Children of Sanchez*, which suggested that the individuals raised in poverty acquire a value system that perpetuates negative behaviors. Deficit theory builds on this belief by assuming that the poor are poor because of their own personal or cultural deficiencies. In a 2008 article in Educational Leadership, Volume 65, author Paul Gorski counters some of this perspective.

The **Family Independence Initiative (FII)** was formed in 2001. More information is available at www.fii.org.

Martin Luther King, Jr.'s letter from the Birmingham jail can be found at a number of sites including www.africa.upenn.edu/Articles_Gen/Letter_Birmingham.html

Underclass is defined by the Merriam Webster dictionary as "a social class made up of people who are very poor and have very little power or chance to improve their lives."

1999 State of the Union Address included invitations to Sammy Sosa and Rosa Parks. www.presidency.ucsb.edu/sou_gallery.php.

Oakland Private Industry Council. Founded in 1978, the Oakland Private Industry Council's mission is to provide accessible, high- quality training and employment services to local residents and employers. www.oaklandpic.org

Social capital has a number of meanings but is included here to highlight the role of relationships that can be of benefit. One source is www.socialcapitalresearch.com/literature/definition.html

Chapter One

Accion was the primary Spanish language newspaper in Nogales, Mexico. Nogales was split by the U.S. Mexican border. On the American side it was Nogales, Arizona, and on the Mexican side Nogales, Sonora.

Minimum wage. In 2017, the federal minimum wage was $7.25 per hour, and has not increased since 2009. Some U.S. states have a higher minimum wage rate. This is listed on the U.S. Department of Labor website, www.dol.gov. The inability to get above poverty in a minimum wage job is included in this article: www.pewresearch.org/fact-tank/2014/02/18/minimum-wage-hasnt-been-enough-to-lift-most-out-of-poverty-for-decades/

Chapter Two

CFED: *"Getting More from Federal Asset-Building Policies,"* by Lillian Woo and David Buchholz, 2007. Page 1. CFED is a multi-faceted organization working at the local, state and federal levels to create economic opportunity that alleviates poverty. www.cfed.org

Poverty level income. In 2017, the U.S. Department of Health and Human Services defined 100% of Poverty (commonly known as the poverty level) as $11,880 for a family of one, $16,020 for a family of two, $20,160 for a family of three and $24,300 for a family of four. This is listed at www.hhs.gov.

Welfare queens. "Welfare queen," is a pejorative term popularized by Ronald Reagan beginning in 1976, used to describe low-income American women who allegedly collect welfare benefits through fraud. Rebuttals can be found in the 2015 Atlantic article titled, *"The Welfare Queen is a Lie,"* by Rachel Black as well as Pulitzer Prize-winning journalist David Zucchino, whose 1997 book *The Myth of the Welfare Queen*, documents impoverished Philadelphia mothers' experiences with the welfare system.

The census bureau studies cited include the following: www.census.gov/content/dam/Census/library/publications/2014/demo/p60-249.pdf

www.census.gov/content/dam/Census/library/publications/2015/demo/p60-252.pdf

www.census.gov/prod/2010pubs/p60-238.pdf

www.census.gov/prod/2005pubs/p60-229.pdf

And a newsroom press release summarizes that poverty is *"primarily a temporary condition"* can be found at: www.census.gov/newsroom/releases/archives/poverty/cb11-49.html

Huffington Post. "How Long Do People Stay on Public Benefits?" by Arthur Delaney, 2015. www.huffingtonpost.com/2015/05/29/public-benefits-safety-net_n_7470060.html

Generational poverty is considered to be when a family's economic level remains below the poverty level income threshold for two or more generations or from 40 to 60 years. The census studies cited here indicate that only around 3% stay under the poverty level for even 3 or 4 years, therefore generational poverty is the exception.

Donald Trump: There was a lot of media coverage of the possibility that Donald Trump used tax loop holes. One article is: *"Donald Trump Used Legally Dubious Method to Avoid Paying Taxes,"* by David Barstow, Mike McIntire, Patricia Cohen, Susanne Craig, and Russ Buettner. New York Times, October 2016.

Chapter Three

Current U.C Berkeley tuition. For the 2017-18 school year, tuition for a full-time UC Berkeley student living in a campus residence hall is $14,068, with room and board estimated at $15,716, for a full cost of $29,784: financialaid.berkeley.edu

Washington Post article. *"Why Poor Kids Don't Stay in College,"* by Jeff Guo. Washington Post, October 2014.

The myth and evolution of the "***model minority***" is captured in Wikipedia with references to other sources.

The book, ***The Free Speech Movement***, by artist and writer, David Lance Goines has a great collection of stories and pictures. "The FSM sparked an unprecedented wave of student activism and involvement." The University of California, www.calisphere.org.

The **War on Poverty** reached its fiftieth anniversary in 2014. Much has been written about it including this piece in the Washington Post by Dylan Mathews: www.washingtonpost.com/news/wonk/wp/2014/01/08/everything-you-need-to-know-about-the-war-on-poverty/?utm_term=.ea65113af52e

The **shooting of Michael Brown** occurred on August 9, 2014, in Ferguson, Missouri. It is chronicled now in Wikipedia with extensive sources and links.

Eighty percent of jobs are filled through social networks. In a 2016 survey conducted by the Adler Group, 85% of survey respondents reported that they got their current job through networking. Louadlergroup.com

Chapter Four

The **Draft** was officially called the **Selective Service System**. The first lottery was held in the summer of 1970 soon after I had to report for duty. Much has been written, not only about the draft, but ways that those with more privileged positions could use to get around it, including continuing their education if they could afford it.

Union Carbide Corporation owned the Linde Division, focused on air products. It had a plant in Pittsburgh, California. I was assigned as plant engineer there but was soon drafted and had to leave my job.

G.I. Bill includes educational benefits that are still available. More information can be found at http://benefits.va.gov/gibill/

Dance Mama Dance: You can see the video on YouTube at www.youtube.com/watch?v=aj4aZfXTz6s

NOTES

Chapter Five

Asian Neighborhood Design. Asian Neighborhood Design (AND), a 501(c)(3) non-profit architecture, community planning, employment training organization with the mission of reducing poverty, revitalizing neighborhoods, and helping disadvantaged individuals and communities become self-sufficient. www.andnet.org

The Golden Dragon massacre is chronicled in Wikipedia along with references to some of the original articles of the incident. wikipedia.org/wiki/Golden_Dragon_massacre. This story is recounted in the San Francisco chronicle's 2016 article by Tim O'Rourke, *"Golden Dragon Massacre, 39 years later."*

Barry Fong-Torres. This story is recounted in the Los Angeles Times article, *"Gang Terrorism Rises in S.F.'s Chinatown,"* from 1972.

CETA, the Comprehensive Employment and Training Act, funded what were referred to as workforce development programs. This legislation was followed by the JTPA, Job Training Partnership Act, and more recently the WIA, the Workforce Investment Act. All have been critical of previous legislation but essentially fund similar programs.

Chapter Six

Control group evaluations. "A control group is an untreated research sample against which all other groups or samples in the research is compared." Although some evaluators stress the importance of using a control group in evaluations, when it comes to addressing issues of poverty some may argue that deliberately using a control group — or people who receive no services or resources via the tested initiative — is ethically questionable.

A poll done by CNN in 2015 on racism. *"Is racism on the rise? More in the U.S. say it's a 'big problem,'* CNN/KFF poll finds," Catherine E. Shoicnet, November 2015.

Newt Gingrich has a history of making denigrating remarks and some can be found in this Media Matters article: mediamatters.org/research/2010/09/13/newt-gingrichs-history-of-bigoted-remarks/170574

Washington Post Live: Video of this panel from March 7, 2013 can be found at www.washingtonpost.com/postlive/panel-safety-nets-reducing-poverty-increasing-economic-mobility. The video also features panelists Ron Haskins, Irwin Redlener, and Jared Bernstein.

Bill O'Reilly quote. Said on air during *The O'Reilly Factor* on Fox News, May 15, 2015.

Drive by Daniel Pink. *Drive: The Surprising Truth About What Motivates Us*. Daniel H. Pink. Riverhead Books, 2011.

Scarcity: *The New Science of Having Less and How it Defines Our Lives* was written by Sendhil Mullainathan and published in 2014.

"*Poverty Interrupted: Applying Behavioral Science to the Context of Chronic Scarcity*," is a white paper written by Allison Daminger, Jonathan Hayes, Anthony Barrows, and Josh Wright, and published by ideas42 in 2015. ideas42 is an organization that uses experimental scientific research to promote scalable solutions for policy and program change.

Whitehall Studies have been going on for decades and much has been written around this research. Wikipedia has references and links to much of the related research: wikipedia.org/wiki/Whitehall Study

Chapter Seven

Iu Mien in America. For more about the Iu Mien in America, read *"To Inherit the Moving Mountains: The Displacement of Iu-Mien Culture and Identity in Refugee America,"* by Catalina Chao, written and published in the 2008-2009 edition of *Prized Writing*.

Internalized racism is loosely defined as the internalization by people of racist attitudes towards members of their own ethnic group, including themselves. This can include the belief in ethnic stereotypes relating to their own group.

Penn State Black Caucus President Holman quote. This quote was featured in the Penn State Collegian's article, *"The impact of prejudice on society"* by Lucie Couillard in September 2013.

Peter Suber quote. Peter Suber's essay *"Paternalism"*, originally appeared in *Philosophy of Law: an Encyclopedia*, Christopher B. Gray (editor) Garland Publishing Company, 1999, II.632-635

Chapter Eight

Skin in the game. Skin in the game is a term coined by renowned investor Warren Buffett referring to a situation in which high-ranking insiders use their own money to buy stock in the company they are running. To have "skin in the game," is to incur risk through involvement in achieving a goal.

The **Black Wall Street** refers to the Greenwood neighborhood in Tulsa, Oklahoma, which housed one of the most successful Black economies in American history. The Oklahoma Historical Society, among others have information on these collective successes that have been ignored.

Bootstrap. The term bootstrap is used to describe using one's own ingenuity rather than external resources to make progress, i.e. to "pull oneself up by one's bootstraps."

Strong and weak ties. These interpersonal bonds are described as holding society together. These relationships also come up in research around social networks.

Chapter Nine

Cambodian owned donut shops spread through-out California. The phenomenon traced its origin to one owner Ted Ngoy. Some general information is available at http://kore. am/the-back-story-behind-cambodian-owned-donut-shops/, as well as a NY Times article from 1995: www.nytimes.com/1995/05/26/us/long-beach-journal-from-cambodia-todoughnut-shops.html

Positive deviance are actions that emerge naturally from a community of peers. It should not be confused with solutions brought into a community by those outside of those communities. Positivedeviance.org compiles some of the stories.

The **Save the Children** effort to help the Vietnamese government improve nutrition for children is well documented. The story as told by the researcher, Jerry Sternin, can be found at www.positivedeviance.org/about_pd/Monique%20VIET%20NAM%20CHAP-TER%20Oct%2017.pdf

Diffusion of innovation theory includes the concepts of positive deviants and early adopters. More can be found at www.ou.edu/deptcomm/dodjcc/groups/99A2/theories. htm

Additional information on the "**chasm**" or waiting period before something will reach a tipping point, can be found at: adscovery.com/2007/08/27/chasm-and-the-tipping-point/ "*Tipping Point*" my Malcolm Gladwell and "*The Speed of Trust*" by Stephen R. Covey, are both popular books on these issues.

Chapter Ten

Theory of Change is a methodology for planning, participation, and evaluation that is used in the philanthropy, Wikipedia provides references and links that document this methodology.

Bernard "Bernie" Madoff is a former stockbroker, investment advisor, and financier. He was convicted of fraud when many wealthy investors lost life savings investing with him.

Village Bottoms is an area in West Oakland, CA. Some of the efforts taking place around 2009 are covered in a CNN report that can be found at http://theblackhour.blog-spot.com/2009/08/rebirth-of-village-bottoms-with-marcel.html

The California Endowment is one of the largest public philanthropic foundations in the

United States. Its mission is to promote the health of all Californians. More information is available on its web site: www.calendow.org/

Updated progress data for families participating in FII can be found on their web site: www.fii.org

Chapter Eleven

Video produced by the Heron Foundation that discusses **FII and it's data collection** can be found on YouTube at www.youtube.com/watch?v=Ke0EnWDWDzo among other videos.

A white paper by the **evaluation** firm, See Change, covers issues of *"social signaling"* as a major factor in the progress documented by participating FII families. That paper is available at www.fii.org/wp-content/uploads/2014/01/Intrinsic-Motivation.pdf

UpTogether, FII's networking site can be found at www.uptogether.org/. However, it is open only to enrolled families or staff.

This **family's story** can be found in an article in Fast Company written by Kim Syman. It can be found at www.fastcoexist.com/3040671/the-power-of-data-to-create-powerful-change

Chapter Twelve

HUD Study No. 15-14 by Brian Sullivan was released in February of 2015 and can be found at https://archives.hud.gov/news/2015/pr15-014.cfm.

The **Urban Institute** was founded in 1968 to understand the problems facing America's cities and assess the programs of the war on poverty.

The Urban Institute study referred to is titled ***Informal and Nonstandard Employment in the United States***" released in August 2011, was written by Demetra Smith Nightingale and Stephen Wandner and can be found at www.urban.org/research/publication/informal-and-nonstandard-employment-united-states

The **Social Compact** studies cited were referred to as Drill Down studies intended to "reveal the hidden strengths of traditionally undervalued communities." The Social Compact web site is www.socialcompact.org/

Percent of state and local taxes paid by quintile in Michigan was used as an example and holds for most states. The source: *Who Pays? A distributional analysis of the tax systems in all 50 states*, 3d edition, Institute on Taxation and Economic Policy.

International Business Times, May 2015 Middle- and low-income Americans are facing far higher state and local taxes than the wealthy, according to a new report assessing tax data from all 50 states. In all, the analysis by the nonpartisan Institute on Taxation and Economic Policy (ITEP) finds that the poorest 20 percent of households pay on average more than twice the effective state and local tax rate (10.9 percent) as the richest 1 percent of taxpayers (5.4 percent).

More about "*affordable housing*" can be found on the Department of Housing and Urban Development web site: https://portal.hud.gov/hudportal/HUD?src=/program_offices/comm_planning/affordablehousing/

Chapter Thirteen

Data analytics may be an unknown area of expertise for nonprofits, but there are a growing number of consultants and businesses eager to help.

Much of the **FII data** referred to here can be found on their web site or in their reports and writings. www.fii.org

Social Innovation is defined as a novel solution to a social problem that is more effective, efficient, sustainable, or just than current solutions.

CPSIA information can be obtained
at www.ICGtesting.com
Printed in the USA
LVOW10s0201280817

546615LV00001B/61/P